LIMITLESS

11 STRATEGIES TO MASTER LIFE AND CAREER

TITILOPE FAKUADE

ISBN: 978-0-578-85590-5
Printed by Power Of Purpose Publishing
www.PopPublishing.com
Atlanta, Ga. 30326

ACKNOWLEDGEMENT

I will like to dedicate this book first and foremost to God, who has been the creative mastermind in everything I do, and to my family particularly my husband and children who are a continual source of inspiration to me.

I will also like to recognize all the people I have worked with throughout my career journey - mentors, mentees, colleagues, family and friends. Special thanks for being a part of this journey. You have in one way or the other shaped it.

Thanks to everyone I had the opportunity to lead, be led by or watch their leadership, thank you for being an inspiration.

My coach and self publishing team. You turned my idea finally into a book. Thank you.

I can't wait to continue to impact lives. The best is yet to come!

INTRODUCTION

Over the years, as I have listened to professionals share the various challenges they face in their lives and careers, some of the questions they asked include:

- How can I grow within an organization?
- What is the future of my career?
- How can I gain greater visibility?
- How will I know my worth?
- Am I the best?
- Why is time never enough?
- Why do I have to work so hard?
- How do I overcome challenges?
- How do I manage high and low moments when they occur?
- Why have I remained stagnant on a role and what can I do about it?
- How can I better manage my relationships with people?
- How can I become the best version of myself?
- How can I live an impactful life?

These are some of the realities that confront working professionals. These questions are constantly on their minds at different stages of their lives and career, whether they are at the undergraduate, entry, or executive level. While thinking about these questions is normal, complaining without a plan or taking proactive action will leave you with no tangible results. It is therefore important to take steps to build a truly intentional and impactful life.

I believe that there are practical answers to these questions with actionable insights. You can be a master of your life and career. I have a knack for always finding the best in everything while remaining focused. Practicing this as an executive has yielded results for me and the people around me. I have a track record of bringing out the best in people and letting them see themselves in a new light while they shape better outcomes for their lives. In the course of my career, I have:

- Coached people to see value in themselves.
- Created opportunities to challenge and grow others.
- Inspired and unleashed potential in people they never imagined existed.
- Unlocked leadership potential.
- Transformed lives positively.
- Executed impossible turnarounds.
- Transformed teams with low morale into happy and engaged teams.
- Built highly motivated and successful teams.

Through these experiences I have developed practical methods to unleash the greatness within people, and I will be sharing these strategies in an easy-to-read format, with personal examples, to unlock your leadership potential.

There is no limit to what we can achieve, and there is no such thing as a perfect life. We all navigate and evolve as we progress in life. We are all on a journey and should be ready to learn, unlearn and relearn. We learn new things by adding new skills and knowledge to what we already know. We unlearn by doing away with old ways of thinking, and we relearn by learning again. On this continuous journey, we need to trust the process and expect great results. And on top of all this, we need to acknowledge the place of the supernatural in everything we do.

My hopes for the reader are that you will gain fresh value adding insights from this book and proceed to use it practically to enhance your career and all spheres of life.

Titilope Fakuade

WHY YOU SHOULD READ

Do you want to live a transformed life, be a leader and inspire the next generation of leaders? Then this book, which is aimed at inspiring readers to become self-aware and to bring out the best in themselves, is for you. It is a personal effectiveness handbook for discovery and leadership focused on success and creating value in life, career, and relationships. Success in any endeavour is relative, and it starts with defining what success means to you.

CONTENTS

CHAPTER 1
IT STARTS WITH THE MIND

Imagine a man who suddenly inherits a piece of land and in his excitement rushes out to plant maize seeds, expecting to yield a harvest in three to four months. The man did not ensure that the soil was adequately prepared and did not apply any fertilizer to it before, during, or after planting. There was no water source to irrigate the farm, leaving it to the uncertain mercy of the weather. With no clear demarcation of his farmland, pedestrians walked over it indiscriminately, using it as a thoroughfare, and with no pest management measures in place, the maize plants that grew were attacked by soil insects and other pests. After four months, there would be no harvest, meaning that his efforts were a waste of resources, time, and money.

Your mind can be likened to the soil in the farm, and it is the foundation of everything you do. You must make sure your mind is adequately prepared and guarded for the success you desire. Just as the farmer needed fertilizer and an irrigation system for his farm, you need to feed your mind with value-adding content to constantly stretch it, even as you permit only the inputs that align with your goals to reside in your mind.

i. Why Your Mind is Important

Your mind is very powerful. Because it shapes your thinking and how you evolve, it needs to be guarded jealously. The thoughts in your mind are responsible for almost everything that happens in your life. With your mind, you can create success or failure, and opportunities or challenges through positive or negative thinking or thoughts. In general, positive thoughts allow you to focus on the good in every situation. You will see examples showing the importance of the mind and positive thoughts as you read on. The journey of life does not mean you will not have negative thoughts. However, as a focused individual, you need to be deliberate in countering these thoughts. You can define methods to ensure that when negative thoughts arise, you apply a neutralizer to stop them from growing further. In the rest of the chapter I will be sharing various strategies that will help you deal with negative thoughts.

Thoughts can be generated through influence. Never underestimate the power of influence be it negative or positive. The influences that shape you have to be properly identified and classified, and if they are negative you need to develop a clear plan to address them. Negative influences need to be carefully studied so that we can transform our lives positively. Identification is the first step, and once this is done, the next step is to develop an improvement plan.

Self-esteem, Focus, and Confidence: Your mind is the foundation to a great life. It can determine your self-esteem, perspectives, and your focus to achieve results. Remember the story of the race between the tortoise and the hare to determine who was faster? About halfway through the race, the hare went to sleep because he considered the tortoise slow, and he did not anticipate the tortoise winning the race. The tortoise on the other hand, continued his slow and steady pace, expecting to win the race. By the time the hare woke up, it was too late. The tortoise had won the race.

So, it is with human life. Our minds, being powerful, need to be fed and conditioned to achieve our desired aim. Our minds enable us to have confidence in our ability and worth. To boost confidence, we need to push through self-limiting beliefs, talk to ourselves, and use positive thoughts to overcome negative thoughts. If, for instance, you feel you are not capable of delivering a task, you will focus more on your fear rather than on how to deliver the task. However, if you believe that you can deliver a task, you will seek out ways to achieve the desired goal. Your attitude becomes a bedrock for subsequent deliveries; if you deliver one task, you develop the confidence to attempt more complex tasks.

While working some years ago as a manager, I had to present a topic on Digital Transformation to the executive team. I was scared since it was my first presentation to this audience, being a group of cross-functional senior business leaders within the organization. Delivering value to the audience will determine the acceptance of the content I was to present and the ensuing contribution and impact on set business objectives. I also needed to make sure this engagement portrayed the value that me and my team bring to the organization. I was so worried about the content to be shared. I wondered about the completeness of the content. Was the information enough and will it be received well; will questions be asked that I will not be able to answer? I also worried about how to deliver it in an engaging manner, the audience had diverse experiences and I had to make sure the content resonated with each subject area. I had to think through how to design and deliver my presentation to buttress my request to the audience. Until I dealt with the fear, I could not focus on my subject. I had to shift my mind by reinforcing my value, past achievements and by reminding myself that I was selected to make the presentation because I am capable. "Yes, I am capable," I said to myself. I must have displayed attitudes at work that portrayed me as suitable.

Once I set my mind to work, everything started falling in place. I became more confident since I was better prepared mentally to deliver the presentation and I had gained the required knowledge in that specific area to add value. I structured my content and finalized the presentation using a good storyline. On the day I was scheduled to deliver the presentation, I ensured I was dressed in comfortable clothing and arrived at the venue promptly just to ensure technology glitches do not affect the experience. It was well delivered, there were multiple questions and clarifications which I had to respond to. I did not focus on the position or superiority of the audience but rather about the topic of discussion. I received feedback after the session from multiple stakeholders about my delivery. It was very well received. At the onset, who would have thought I could stand for over 45mins to defend a position, address concerns as they arose, and remain composed.

Your mind is a very important success factor that shapes who you become and how you achieve your goals

Shift Your Perspectives: Your view of life determines the outcomes you observe. Is the cup half-full or half-empty? Do you view things as half-full, which implies a positive outlook or half-empty, which implies a negative outlook? You can appraise a situation in different ways depending on your point of view. Do you see problems as challenges or opportunities for growth? Have you been passed over for a promotion or have you been stuck in the same role for donkey years, and do you see either situation as missed opportunities or opportunities to explore new things? Being passed over for a promotion could be an opportunity to develop new skills or spend more time with family, things you have been longing to do but couldn't because of your busy schedule. Shift your viewpoint to the positive and see the difference. You will say hello to wonderful beginnings once you begin to shift your perspectives.

In the early days of my career, out of fifteen(15) trainees employed within an Information and Communication Technology organization, I was the only engineer remaining with the organization after five years while all the other trainees had left, some left immediately after the one year trainee program while others left at different stages, some to study abroad, some secured higher positions in other organizations. Although I had the opportunity and exposure to various complex projects within banking, oil and gas, telecoms, IT and different businesses, with the opportunity to engage industry players, I kept feeling left out that I was the only engineer of my set. After about four years specifically when I returned to the office from an offsite posting of over one year, I was determined to focus on the positives. I continued to give my best on the role, changed my wardrobe to reflect I was ready for a change while seeking opportunities for a change. When I least expected it, there was an opportunity to apply to a prestigious multinational company for an engineer role. I was not selected at the interview and got an opportunity for another role. The interview went well and the rest is history. I secured a new role in a multinational company after waiting for so long. Imagine if I had become dejected and not given my best at the ICT organization, my mind would not have been prepared for the interviews and subsequent appointment. Who is contributing to your mindset?

ii. Feed Your Mind

What you feed your mind is equally important. Thoughts, ideas, knowledge, words, and confessions or what you say, play an important role in how your mind grows. One negative thought, if not addressed, can lead to so many other negative thoughts that build up into stories, which shape your outlook about a situation or a person. Negative utterances, like I'm no good, I always fail, and so on, will affect your outlook on life. ...

What do you see, positives or negatives? If you constantly look for the negatives in every situation, you will see negatives all the time rather than the bright side of life. Without an objective assessment of a situation, you will hold grudges against people, which, most times, is not worth the trouble and which, has a negative impact on your outlook on people and life in general.

I believe it is crucial to apply objectivity in assessing situations, and it starts with your mind. What are you feeding your mind? How are you guarding your mind? What thoughts are you allowing to grow in your mind? Shaping your thoughts and devising plans to address issues promptly is one key step to great progress in life.

iii. Develop a Growth Mindset

Achievements are not totally dependent on hard work or talent. Your thoughts and beliefs drive your behaviors and actions, which then become your visible results. Therefore, you need to develop a growth mindset.

A growth mindset helps you to view mistakes and failures as opportunities and lessons learnt because each experience is an avenue to grow your mind.

To develop a growth mindset, you have to be deliberate regarding what you think about and avoid negative thoughts by consciously replacing them with positive thoughts. You can also develop a culture of speaking affirmations aloud daily to avoid negative thoughts. Consider making affirmations such as:

- I am great and can figure things out once I set my mind to do so.
- I have been successful in little tasks; therefore, I can handle bigger tasks.
- Even if I am stuck, I will get support from others.
- I can handle a difficult customer or stakeholder today by objectively addressing their issues.
- I will think the best of myself and everyone today.

These are some examples that can be expanded depending on your specific needs. Gradually, you will see yourself living out your affirmations because your mind would have been conditioned for success. I have seen instances of people transforming themselves and achieving massive feats, despite fear from within, because of their daily affirmations.

In the tortoise and hare story I shared earlier, the tortoise was not afraid of failure otherwise, he would not have accepted to run the race, neither was he complacent because he kept on with the race. The need for a growth mindset can therefore not be overemphasized to ensure your success and greatness in life.

iv. Conditioning Your Mind

Your mind must be conditioned for success. Conditioning requires a reinforcement of your mind through repetition. To achieve the desired results, it must be done consistently.

Imagine that you committed to exercise your body for fifteen minutes daily over a period of one month. If you start the exercise without maintaining consistency, you are not conditioning your mind to pull through and achieve set goals. If someone else with the same goal stayed committed throughout the one-month period then that person would be better conditioned for success because of the discipline and consistency involved in exercising daily for a month. His or her mind would have been trained. So it is with life, if you do not train your mind to shift and think positively, it is easy to derail and lose focus. Your mindset affects every area of life.

Believe in Yourself: You need to believe in yourself and this starts from your mind. Although you might feel you have not achieved much, get the small things right and start taking stock. There is no need to compare yourself with others because everyone is on a personal journey and our experiences shape our unique selves. The fact that some of your mates or colleagues have progressed faster than you have in your industry does not mean you are a failure. The fact that you do not have a first-class degree should not stop you from becoming the best. Even if you have been at a position for five years without a promotion, it should not stop you from being the best. Your mind plays a major role in your ability to believe in yourself.

Dealing with Challenges and Fears: Challenges, fears, and uncertainties are part of life. However, you need to develop courage in the face of fear, making your moves while addressing your fears as you make progress. Stop being afraid of what could go wrong, rather focus on what can go right. You need to harness your mind to focus on the positive. No one has everything figured out. Most times you do not even know what to fully expect when embarking on a new idea. You have to continuously improve your plan as you progress.

There is no limit to what we can achieve, the only limitation we have is in our mind. As you progress in reading this book, you will see stories of how achievements happened when the mind is well prepared, and self-doubt is not allowed to be a hindrance. Deep inside of you is a person no one knows yet. As you evolve, you will discover a new you with new capabilities you never knew existed. Once you surmount a challenge, you become experienced in that area and can handle more responsibilities or more complex situations. Do not shrink your brilliance. The world is waiting for you.

Limiting Beliefs: Although we might have been conditioned over the years because of limiting beliefs, it is possible to change this mindset and condition our minds for success. This requires a deliberate effort to acknowledge that there will be uncertainties and to focus your energy on things within your control. Limiting beliefs can be surmounted once you make up your mind to let them go, although it might not be immediate and will require a process. The belief that only certain people can achieve heights in their careers or that I am not good enough, is an example of a limiting belief. These kinds of beliefs hold you back from fulfilling your purpose.

To overcome limiting beliefs, you need to pause and reflect on all areas of your life to identify them. Realize that the limiting thoughts are not true and take your power back. Stop blaming others for your results and remain accountable to yourself. This is an important goal to work on.

Within organizations, vision boards are placed in strategic locations to showcase the values, core beliefs or any other vital information that can shape the culture of the organization. You can apply this approach to your life because you condition your mind with what you see consistently. Do you have a vision board that shows the changes you desire? Is it a picture of what you want to achieve or the qualities you want to see in yourself and others? Your vision board is a visual representation of your desires, which can be placed in locations you always visit, like your bedroom, bathroom, or living room. It can be written as text or it can be a collage of images and pictures of your desired states. You can place names or photos of role models you want to emulate or affirmations to be read daily, which will serve as a source of inspiration and motivation. A friend of mine had health challenges which required that he shed some weight in order to become fit and healthy. At the beginning of the year, he made a vision board with a slimmer version of himself and placed it on the door to his kitchen, he made it a screensaver on his phones, this way it becomes visible whenever he visits the kitchen or attempts to eat anything. His goal was to lose 10kg within the year. He prepared and placed a meal plan on his refrigerator, installed a fitness app on his phone to support and track his progress. He was tempted at different occasions to give up but whenever he saw the vision board and all the pointers he had, he remained focused. This guided his eating habits, conditioned him to practice disciplined eating habits. While reviewing the year, he was very excited that he had attained his goal. If he had not taken time to document his plans, things might not have turned out positive. He has since used this approach to achieve his goals. Within organizations, I have seen the impact of vision boards on individual behaviors and culture.

These vision boards are placed across walkways or meeting rooms visible to everyone within the organization, while walking on the corridors and waiting for meetings to commence. Individuals look at the vision board to read the inscriptions, by stopping on the walkway or while waiting for a meeting to begin. People start living out the writings or pictures placed. It formed daily actions and culminated in achieving set objectives. Each day presents an opportunity to become the best version of yourself. Do not waste it.

v. Your Environment Matters

Your environment is a key contributing influence to your success. From the moment when you wake up, you are confronted by loads of distractions - technology wakes you up, then you pick up your phone to check the time and the next thing you know, you are bombarded with social media distractions: WhatsApp, Facebook, and LinkedIn messages start popping up. Some of these distractions sneak in subtly and before you realize it, you are in neck-deep. Imagine visiting a website to obtain information and as is common, another recommended article pops up while reading. If you are not deliberate about your choices, you would click on the article and be redirected, and on and on. However, all these distractions can be avoided.

To change yourself, you need to make incremental changes within your environment that are beneficial and would act as triggers for a mindset shift. It could be scheduling time on your calendar for social media catch-up to avoid wasting time on social media. Music is also a good influence that can shape your mind. It is therapeutic and good for the soul. Are you always busy with no time to spare for quietness during the day? Do you need a quiet environment? Depending on your personality, you may have to be deliberate in curating the kind of environment that suits you.

Renewing the mind is a gradual process and requires conditioning using the steps (so far) highlighted. Once, as a young graduate I was assigned to provide IT support at an off-site organization. My senior colleague who was working on the project with me, was the project lead with more knowledge and resigned within two weeks of our resumption. Naturally, I was afraid because I was unsure about my ability to deliver the tasks, required support, and other deliverables that were expected seeing that I was suddenly the only resource at the site. Recruiting a replacement for him was not an immediate solution and there was a need to defend my reputation as an engineer to this esteemed organization.

The first thing I did to quell my fears was to recondition my mind. I had to tell myself that I had what it took to get the job done. Then I equipped myself by reading manuals to broaden my knowledge base. This gave me insight on a range of possibilities and my deliverables began to seem less daunting. Whenever fear or doubts threatened my confidence, I would go back to the online library to learn more. I had to research discussion groups and fora online where you could see how others had solved similar problems. As an engineer, problem solving was the norm.

By the time I was leaving the site, I received a commendation and a note that stated that whoever was coming to replace me, must have undergone the same level of training and exposure that I had. Unknown to the organization I had been assigned to,

I had not gone through any formal training, rather, I had challenged my mind to step up my game. We have the capacity to renew our mind.

Places You Visit: The places you visit and the people you relate or hang out with determine how your mind evolves. You degrade your values if you constantly visit places that do not add any value to you and do not align with your goals. This is why it is important to define your goals, dreams, and values so that wherever you choose to visit are places that align with them. As an industry professional, you cannot spend your time on chatter or rumor mongering all day and expect positive outcomes. This also applies to how much time you spend on various activities. Planning and focus need to be taken seriously to avoid wasting too much time on what will not add any value.

Who are The People Around You?: We are as good as the people who are around us. Who do you surround yourself with? Surround yourself with people that will bring out the best in you. Having friends who are aligned with your thinking and growth plans is a factor that will fuel and condition your mind. You will have common discussion points when you hang out with these friends, and you can challenge each other towards your goals. This is not about competition; it is a way of inspiring and supporting each other as friends. This does not imply an over-reliance on friends because it is important to be self-motivated. Hence, we are having this discussion about your mind and its importance.

Friends and mentors shape your mind, and your engagement with them can include both physical and virtual meetings. As the world evolves, we are no longer limited by physical meetings, we can now leverage on virtual connections. These connections can take place anywhere in the world, exposing you to global thought leadership and experiences. You can engage your virtual connections using technology on LinkedIn, any other social media channel or collaboration tools such as Teams or Zoom. Do you realize that the content you consume online shapes your thoughts and therefore, who you become? Who are your online friends across all channels? Are you leveraging the power of virtual connections for good?

vi. Key Reflections

Just as we take vitamins and supplements to protect ourselves from common colds, so it is important to take deliberate steps to guard our minds and how they evolve. The outcome and experiences of your life are expressions of what you believe or do not believe. Your words do matter, so if you look around you with a desire for things to become better, then say or speak it. Be bold and declare what you want to experience. You are the CEO of your life and career. You must change your beliefs to have a good life trajectory. Your daily routine is critical to who you become.

- Your mind is important.
- Your mind is a powerful tool that shapes your future outcomes: success or failure.
- You can and should train your mind to harness its powers.
- How you view life matters; is your cup half-full or half-empty?

Don't just play to try and settle for crumbs, play life expecting to win massively.

CHAPTER 2
YOU ARE A BRAND

What story do people tell about you when you are not in the room? What ways do you provide value? What differentiates you from others? Why are you the best? Why should anyone listen to you? These are some questions that come to mind when discussing your impact and the brand you portray. You need to define how you want to stand out and be valuable. Your brand should be an intentional effort to create and influence public perception of you as an individual. It normally is used to gain credibility and to be seen as authority within an industry. To effectively project your value as part of your brand, you need to make a conscious effort. You must be ready to raise your game and go the extra mile.

i. Your Brand Enables You Standout

Your words define your life, values, and personality, and they are therefore your brand. How you express yourself matters. Your brand is a combination of your skills, personality, and experiences backed by your performance. It is not consistent to communicate a brand value of excellence if it does not show in your deliverables. If you are positioning yourself as an excellent person, we must see excellence in everything you do. There should be a correlation between what you project and what you deliver.

Some thought-provoking key questions an individual can use to develop his or her brand, include: what do I stand for? What motivates me? What is important to me and what can I offer? What am I an expert in? What is my unique value proposition? When you discover how to stand out and showcase your value in an authentic way, people will understand what sets you apart, and you will gain trust and develop authority. Your authority attracts new business or career opportunities. This comes through hard work and recognition by your audience, who believe in your point of view, because they have come to know you as an authority in a particular area. The largest asset you own is the brand called you.

ii. Build Your Brand Intentionally

Your brand is not developed overnight, it has to be consistently and intentionally built. When do you start building your brand? A young graduate who is aware of the importance of this asset also understands that starting early to build his or her brand, in life and career, is crucial because his or her experiences will shape peoples' overall perception of him or her. Your brand is linked to your experiences and interactions with people. Some of these experiences could be work experiences, volunteering experiences, and so on. You should have both an online and offline strategy to determine the content and context you want to project. To build an online brand, you need to be intentional and ensure your content reaches the right audience and communicates to your audience that you can solve their problems.

After I assumed the role of an executive at this multinational telecommunications company, one day I was unexpectedly called to address a lingering challenge. This challenge on data and insights had been lingering for an extended period and was needed to make valuable decisions. Interestingly, someone who was an external member across the group of operations made the comment that now that I had come on the scene, the issue would be solved.

This got me thinking. Why was that comment made? When did I become someone that could solve these kinds of problems even before I had evaluated or analyzed the issue? I realized I had developed a personal brand of being result-oriented and this characteristic had been evident in all my job experiences from the past to the present to enable me become the brand that people see today. Although this brand was developed unconsciously and was based on my values, and consistency being an important component, it nevertheless had translated into 'my' brand. You can be known as someone who would always explore solutions to problems even if they are not 100% perfect. This is the place of offering value.

I have also seen instances where when someone's name is mentioned to lead an initiative, everyone says, "No way, we would prefer that someone else is assigned to deliver the initiative." Is this the kind of brand you want to portray? If not, reassess what you have been projecting so far and take deliberate steps to change the prevailing narrative.

This does not apply only to the workplace; it extends to all areas of life. Can you be trusted to complete a task? As a father or mother, to what degree can you be relied on or not? Is your spouse confident that you will respond to their missed calls or at least communicate through other channels during the day while at work? These tiny actions accumulate to define the brand of you. If you do not define your brand, others will do it for you in their own way.

Develop Your Strategy: As a professional, you must define a strategy to deliberately change your narrative from low to high performance and visibility. This involves evaluating where you are today and the level of visibility you want in future in terms of your reputation and career. Who is your target audience and how will you reach them—through the workplace, industry associations, or social media? Conduct a SWOT (Strengths, Weaknesses, Opportunities, and Threats) analysis to determine your strengths and weaknesses, the opportunities that you can leverage, and threats external to you that can impact your journey. What skills do you need to improve on to aid your goals? Do you want to improve your leadership, public speaking, or writing skills? Are there core competencies or technical skills you need to develop? Can you do this alone or do you require support from a coach?

Providing answers to these questions will enable you to develop a strategy to execute. You can consider getting the support of a coach in crafting and building a reputable brand if you feel you cannot do this alone. Seeking support does not belittle you in any way, rather it indicates how much importance you place on projecting and communicating your identity.

It is Never Too Late: There is no best time to start building your brand. The journey starts once you become aware, no matter how late in your career or life. Starting early gives you an advantage because you can be deliberate and consistent in building your reputation. Anyone who has been portraying the wrong brand and wants to change this, that is, who is interested in a reinvention, can do this with deliberate actions. Your story must be consistent and whatever you project must be defendable. You cannot be two different individuals online and offline (physically). You must continue to build the asset called you through your experiences and actions. Yes, your actions count.

Project or Showcase Yourself: Your identity is not confined to your immediate environment only. I believe in telling your story, so others know about your reputation or whatever image you want to project. You cannot be totally dependent on others to share your stories because they can shape your stories in a way that might not reflect what you desire. This can be likened to how businesses and organizations use various techniques to brand themselves based on their positioning and offerings. Businesses and organizations promote their services to ensure customers have them as top of mind and understand why their services should be patronized rather than that of the competition and other alternatives, leading to huge investments in branding and communications. This is why as an individual and a professional, you need to make deliberate plans to showcase and promote yourself and develop ways to consistently display who you are and what you stand for. Your brand can be about always having a positive attitude and a greeting for colleagues every morning. It can revolve around standing strong and focused while solving complex issues.

While building your brand, you can take up projects that align with your projected brand identity. For example, speaking at conferences or featuring your thought leadership in reputable magazines. Do you speak up in meetings? I used to be very quiet in meetings because I was afraid of speaking up and being wrong. A cross-functional meeting can hold without me uttering a word, despite having many thoughts within me that require clarity or ideas that can add value. I have realized, over the years, that this is a disservice to myself. We are all on a journey of learning, and when I ask questions, I am either contributing to the discussion or seeking clarity, which helps me on my professional journey. Some years ago, I was invited to speak at a conference, this was a platform that could be used as a leverage to showcase my capabilities. It was the largest technology conference in West Africa by TechPoint Africa. Due to fear, I delayed deciding until the last minute when I rejected the offer. On retrospection, I see this as a learning curve, it was an opportunity to project myself outside my organization.

Take Your Brand Outside Your Sphere of Influence: It is important to let others see your brand within and outside your sphere of influence, in your organization or industry. What value do you bring to the table? Spreading your brand outside your usual sphere of influence gives room for growth and opportunities. People are seeking solutions to any number of issues or are trying to recruit new hires to solve specific problems, however, no one will know about you, if you keep your capabilities to yourself. Projecting your brand will create visibility for you and moreover, you will start engaging ideas or solutions you never knew existed because opportunities will seek you out.

This brings us to the discussion about the channel to be used. I think that using both online and offline channels is best. This is because you should build a reputation based on your actions, and experiences and because you also need to be available through online channels to engage with a global audience. The world is now a global space, and you cannot continue to operate locally within your industry or country.

With a solid online presence, you become visible to address global needs, and well positioned for opportunities.

I have, through the LinkedIn platform, been invited to present my thought leadership at various speaking engagements and write articles for digital magazines. In 2020, I was a speaker at Data & Analytics Summit West Africa, an online knowledge-based summit for professionals. I had to speak on Prominence of Data as a Service. I also published an article on Workplace Learning being a key strategy for success and sustainability. It was hinged on the future and the need to be ready to learn, unlearn and relearn. Earlier in the year, I published the digital transformation program I was leading in two reputable magazines - Business Chief Africa and GigaBit Magazine. In 2019, my thought leadership insight was published in CIO magazine, a magazine focused for IT professionals. I discussed 3 strategies for CIO business success with my perspective as an African leader. These opportunities were established through LinkedIn and I have leveraged on these opportunities to further showcase my brand outside my sphere of influence.

These opportunities might not have arisen if I did not have the right presence on that platform.

iii. Build From Your Experiences

You can build your brand deliberately from experiences at work by signifying your intention to lead cross-functional projects, which would give you the additional breadth and allow others to see your impact and value. Embarking on such projects is a good way to disrupt your comfort zone and deliver value, rather than waiting to be made redundant.

I know a couple of people who lead various initiatives within the organization, I used to wonder why and how they combine this with their assigned responsibilities. Over the years, I have become more informed, and I now understand the value of leading these kinds of initiatives as they allow you to stretch, learn across the board, network with more stakeholders, and enjoy so many other benefits. You develop additional skills that you may not have discovered, had you not offered to lead these initiatives. You just need to be cautious to avoid negative impacts on your core responsibilities. As you read further in this book, you will see many examples of how this was established.

Volunteering as a Channel to Develop Your Brand: Volunteering provides opportunities to offer your services to your community. It has immense benefits, including growing your network, stretching beyond your comfort zone because you will have to deal with responsibilities that are not normally within your purview, and making new friends while adding value to the cause of the volunteering group. It can also help you uncover hidden talents. Volunteering builds your reputation and credibility as a subject matter expert and may open up new career opportunities.

By being actively involved in the activities of my secondary school and university alumni associations, I have discovered new capabilities around leading, influencing, organizing, and applying creative energy for ideation and designs. Some years ago, while on vacation, I initiated a group of alumni students through WhatsApp and we started sharing knowledge. With the need to ensure we work together to achieve some common goals while giving back to our alma mater. I began leading, influencing and shaping plans and decisions. In this   process I started cultivating my creativity as I designed programs and communication materials to engage and effectively project a reputable and organized image. As we progressed on this journey, I received feedback from mates on the value add with the opportunity to mentor others.

Sharing your expertise while volunteering, can also lead to new career or business opportunities. In choosing volunteering experiences, you need to consider your passion, avenues to make a difference and add value, which could by supporting a non-profit organization or any other community service. Adding value to any of the programs and initiatives you embark on, would further support the goal of developing your brand identity. Other volunteers would see your capabilities, which they might have been searching for or were not aware they needed until then. By showcasing your skills and capabilities with your strong personal brand, you are shaping yourself for success.

iv. Build For Long-term Success

Your brand can create a good reputation, strong validation, and perpetuity. Your reputation is formed by the opinions held about you by others while validation is the recognition and confirmation by others that your views are respected and useful. Perpetuity refers to your brand lasting for an indefinitely long period. To ensure your brand endures the test of time, you need a strategy.

What are your aims and objectives? Who are you targeting? And how will you evaluate the long-term success of your personal brand? Your brand must tell a story about you, and it is important to build your brand for long-term success.

Reputation: You need to define your brand and live it consistently. Let others tell your story and create a positive impact. All of this will culminate in living a legacy once your reputation is built and others are telling your story. It requires being intentional about the legacy you create. You can build a personal brand for the long haul, and it becomes your legacy. This will further cement your reputation, distinguish you from others, attract new networks or recommendations, thereby promoting visibility and enabling validation through the community that knows you and your brand, as they can give testimonials about you. Your reputation can be so validated by others that it leads to perpetuity because your opinions are considered valid and worthwhile. When you are known for excellence, your reputation speaks for you everywhere you go. Validation is an important measure of your reputation.

A strong personal brand is critical for all professionals and the power to build one is in your hands. You must define your brand, know your value, and take ownership to make it a success.

Validation and Perpetuity: Recently I was one of fifty professionals from across Africa, who received the 2020 Career Influencer award from Workbooth Magazine. The award was given to celebrate individuals who have gone out of their way to support colleagues, associates, and mentees to achieve career excellence and become outstanding professionals. This came as a surprise to me because I didn't know I had been nominated for this award. It, however, is a culmination of all the experiences I have had and created for others over the years, building my reputation while being genuinely interested in the growth of colleagues and team members. Unbeknownst to me, a former team member recognized my efforts and decided to nominate me. The rest is history, as my nomination went through multiple evaluations by seasoned panelists for the final selection as a 2020 African Career Influencer.

Receiving this kind of validation means that others will start telling your story as you become an inspiration to them. You gradually become a role model, charting the path for others who aspire to greater heights.

Your brand applies to all areas of life and not limited to your professional life. It does not have to be stagnant. The fact that you started as an engineer and aspire to become a CEO does not mean your brand cannot be reinvented along your journey. As an engineer or customer-facing employee, your focus will be on achieving results and working with colleagues within a team, communicating your value and positive attitude. As a CEO, your focus will be on shaping the future of the organization while working through people.

You are building a brand, irrespective of your role or position within an organization. I started out my career unaware of some of these things, but I have now evolved to become conscious and deliberate in building and nurturing my personal brand identity.

v. Key Reflections

Key considerations to help you develop a quality brand include understanding your values and understanding why you need a brand.

- When you consistently offer value, you are gradually building a brand for yourself.

- Your brand is a combination of your skills, personality, and experiences backed by your performance.
- It is easier to build a brand based on true passion, showing authenticity rather than trying to create a brand as someone you are not.
- Your authentic self is important on this journey.
- You need to put effort into developing your brand.
- Amplify what is amazing about you and showcase your strengths with authenticity.
- The world needs the special gift of you.

CHAPTER 3
THE POWER OF INTENTIONALITY

The power of intentionality requires you to be deliberate and mindful of your plans and actions. There are no shortcuts to world-class performance. Each day presents an opportunity to design our lives through deliberate steps and actions.

i. Live By Design

Living by design requires us to be mindful and to develop a sense of purpose, which guides our day-to-day activities. Having an overall strategic plan will cause us not to react to events. Being mindful requires you to be aware or conscious about life, its happenings, and your daily activities. It requires you to be aware of your thoughts and emotions. To be mindful, you need to consider taking regular breaks, paying attention to details, and taking a walk while admiring nature. Understanding the purpose of what you are doing will help you develop a sense of purpose. This is a critical element of being deliberate. Having a sense of purpose helps you prioritize your life in a way that takes your uniqueness into consideration.

Seeking new experiences, trying out a new hobby, and shifting from your comfort zone are essential to living by design. This will help alleviate your fears and expand your mind. Don't wait to be driven, but rather live your life with a sense of purpose. Define goals and chart your way to achieving them. An individual with no plan at the beginning of a new year will wander through the year without achieving any goals because there are constant distractions everywhere. Being deliberate requires that you formulate a plan that is in line with your goals and aspirations. This plan can encompass career, family, spiritual growth, health, or any other area of your life. The plan will serve as a guide, which can be actioned and tracked.

Personally and professionally, I have seen this work. I will be sharing as you read, some of the examples where this has been successful. When we set goals and consciously start working towards them, achieving and celebrating milestones become doable.

ii. Be Disciplined and Set Goals

Your career goals could include completing a master's degree within two years. Your family goal could be to schedule family time to enable you to bond better with your family. Perhaps, one family hangout day a week is an action you can take to support your goal of family bonding. Taking care of your health with goals around weight loss helps you become intentional in your food intake and exercise routine. You cannot plan to live a healthy lifestyle and keep wishing it will happen by itself. You need to have a deliberate set of actions, which forms your plan to achieve the healthy lifestyle goal.

A friend of mine wanted to buy a house, but after she made some calculations, she concluded that she could not afford to buy it. Undeterred, she reviewed her options. She analyzed her sources of income which constituted about 30%, She decided to obtain a loan for the remaining 70% required to buy the house. She had an aggressive repayment plan, limited her spending within this duration and ensured she had extra savings. She leveraged her family for support on other areas of spend. This allowed her to generate lump sum payment to the bank at different intervals. She did not rely only on the monthly repayment, this most times includes 90% interest with 10% focused on repaying the initial loan amount. With the lump sum payment, the principal amount was reduced, and she did not have to pay all the intended interest. She ended up paying off the loan in 2 years instead of 10 years as originally planned by the financial institution. The ability to set goals and remain disciplined were critical steps to achieving the result.

This case study can also be applied to your career. You can set goals to complete your MBA or take professional courses to enhance your skills. Following through with this, will position you for career advancement when your preparation meets opportunity. Being deliberate requires you to be forward thinking, to aspire, and to employ discipline to actualize your goals.

iii. Moving From Mediocrity to Greatness

Why remain mediocre when you can become great? Being mediocre is neither good nor bad, it implies something or someone is of ordinary quality while greatness is distinguished and renowned. Why choose mediocrity when there is greatness in you. Decide to impact the world with the rich, valuable, and untapped resources within you. All you need to do is awaken the greatness within as everyone is great at something. You can achieve whatever you choose with excellence and mastery. Being deliberate or intentional provides a platform to move from mediocrity to greatness.

Distractions are Inevitable: Distractions are inevitable and can come in different forms: television, computers, phones, games, friends, busy work schedules, voluntary work, and a host of others. These distractions include using mobile phones, especially at this time when phones are now also work tools. Imagine having your work emails on your phone as well as active social media apps, games, and so on. Without discipline and proper planning, you can continue to browse through various apps while attending to work and then realize that you have spent over twelve hours surfing, without clear progress or achievement.

However, having a deliberate plan enables you to focus, keep track of, and actualize the deliveries stated in your plan. Tracking will enable you to identify when you have deviated from the plan so you can take appropriate steps to address this promptly. Doing this will enable you re-channel your energy to close the gap and realign with your plans. You need to know how to schedule work, phone time, and family catch-up time. You have to wake up each day and be determined to make it great with thoughtful choices.

Win-win During Tough Times: Although there will be tough times, these times do not last. I remember when I resumed a new role in a new environment outside my home country. The business landscape was challenging, there was a new culture to understand and adapt considering it was not my home country. I had new team members to work with, we both need time to understand each other and evolve to a forming team that will deliver results. I was tasked with delivering solid business outcomes. Personally, it was my first time away from family. There were a lot of improvement areas – systems, people and processes and considering it was my first time in this environment, having a plan enabled me to focus and ensure I achieved target goals. I had to identify and clearly articulate all the areas of improvement.

While the challenges persisted, a deliberate plan was drafted to solve the identified issues, it was tracked closely for closure. As new challenges surfaced, the action plan was updated with new changes. All of which was still being tracked effectively.

Tracking and executing well enabled me to achieve tangible results within 1 year. It was a state of continuous improvement and adaptation.

The fact that you have a plan does not mean everything will work according to your plan. You have to continue to adapt your plan to reflect current realities. If you have stayed too long in a particular role, without any form of promotion, you can continue to follow and tweak your career plan while waiting for the next opportunity. Deliberate actions could include taking a training or certification course in your area of expertise to better position you for new opportunities. Your training could even create new opportunities for you. Although your plan indicates that you should have become a manager in two years, the fact that it has not yet materialized should not stop you from updating the plan. There should be continuous evolution of the plan due to various external factors. A win-win is assured during tough times once you are intentional.

Consistency: Consistency is a key attribute required to move from mediocrity to greatness. Consistent hard work leads to success and ultimately greatness. You cannot reach your goals within a defined duration or time with inconsistency. You cannot actualize your plans or they could take a longer time to materialize if you are inconsistent. Once you are doggedly deliberate and develop a habit of being consistent, it becomes easier to achieve your goals. You cannot be deliberate today and then tomorrow waive off your determined approach to thoughtful choices. Practicing consistency over time makes you a better person.

A case in point is speaking up in meetings. Initially, you may experience fear of failure or appearing inexperienced. However, when you overcome your initial fear and consistently speak up in meetings, you will become better at asking questions or making comments. You will gradually become better at giving and receiving feedback, both negative and positive. You can apply the consistency you've developed in one area to other goals.

iv. Embrace Imperfections

You are not perfect and no one who has walked the earth's surface is. Did you think your intentional plan would be perfect? Of course not. You'll observe flaws as you progress and you have to be flexible. Some details might be missing or might not have been well thought out. You need to embrace imperfections. Imperfections in your work make it great. The flaws, broken plans, and our less-than-perfect choices are some of the things that make us unique and memorable. In setting out to find a life partner, we seek perfection, forgetting we are not perfect ourselves. Just as it is in marriage, imperfections exist in our careers and should be embraced. It also applies to all areas of life, be it personal, work and career, family, parenting, or relationships.

If people can relate to your struggles and imperfections, they will be attracted to you and your unique capabilities. These imperfections make us human and further showcase the need for continuous iteration and adaptation. While being intentional, you must also be ready to adapt your plans and constantly make changes depending on the current assessment. Your journey is one of continuous learning. Be comfortable with imperfections and create opportunities to become a better version of yourself.

Some Goals Will be Missed: Achieving plans that you have mapped out is a key success factor to becoming a better version of yourself. Some plans will be achieved while others will not be achieved. It is completely normal to miss some planned achievements. The most important thing is to ensure progress is happening and you are not stagnant. If you plan to achieve more visibility through speaking up and adding value, you might not be able to consistently follow through with the plan due to various reasons. Fear might still hold you back even when you do not expect it to. The key to addressing this, is practice. Practice makes perfect. Begin at the first meeting where you break the jinx and gradually continue to speak up. Become more conscious that you plan to speak up, and seek opportunities to speak up and communicate your ideas rather than keeping them to yourself. Sometimes your input, which you think is not valuable, could help with charting a new initiative or addressing a problem.

An important step to gaining relevance and moving from mediocrity to greatness, is to have a plan to address pain or focus areas. Review and identify your pain or focus areas and build a plan to address and close any gaps identified. Your intentionality is what will enable you to overcome issues or achieve your goal. By being intentional, your actions are coordinated to achieve an overall goal, which might not be visible to others.

Progress Counts: Every step counts. It is crucial to acknowledge every bit of progress that you make. Consider the goal of speaking up in meetings that we discussed earlier. After you speak up in the first meeting, you will gradually gain confidence, which you can use to learn how to improve at the next meeting. It is important to speak up even if your voice shakes. Do not let fear keep you quiet. Acknowledge your progress no matter how small it is because it will motivate you to continue speaking up. You can contribute a sentence during your first attempt and as your confidence grows, you would contribute more effectively with multiple sentences and spread across multiple areas of expertise.

Some Areas Will Not be Perfect: There was a time I was struggling to complete my MBA due to demanding work pressures. We were only two available team members in a team of six, actively working on projects and various deliveries. I had to deal with multiple stakeholders with complex requirements and varying urgency needs, with everyone wanting immediate response or attention. At the same time, I was registered for my MBA program at University of Wale, UK. I could not take any course for a year due to this pressure. I reflected and realized the impact of this decision. The fear of not attaining my goal as originally planned brought me back to reality considering money had been expended. One day, I decided things were going to change because I needed to complete the program.

I had begun the MBA because I needed to build a business mindset and develop leadership and strategic skills required to shape my career growth. I was determined to meet my goal as my initial enthusiasm had been disrupted due to other priorities.

I commenced engaging the materials again. I started reading them and ensured all my assignments were duly turned in, developed a plan to ensure I completed everything within the year. It was tough. I could not consistently meet up with all the demands associated with MBA coupled with work and the home front. Family time was impacted sometimes.

With a plan in place to ensure that I complete one module per quarter, I started staying up late or waking up early to catch up on schoolwork. I continued working at my job during the day. It was a tough season, but for a limited period. Completing the various modules, surveys, and research, which culminated in presenting my project dissertation was only achievable as a result of an intentional plan and consistency. Distractions abounded, but I embraced my imperfections when I could not achieve the targets that I had set, and I acknowledged the progress I made. I did not quit, but kept on with my plan.

There was a request from the head of department to a team of 10 people soliciting comments about what the future offers and how we should prepare. I provided input which was selected to become an initiative. I was tasked with development of a vision board. Initially, I had concerns and almost started regretting why I had provided input to the discussion, because I was now saddled with the responsibility of crafting a vision board for the department. I did not know where to begin because my work schedule was still tight. I delayed starting anything for about five months, until one day, at another meeting, my team pointed out that our vision board was pending because of me. Right there, I crafted a plan of action to form a team of individuals to join me on the journey. The team and I brainstormed the design and finally the vision board was completed. It was a first of its kind, submitted in both physical and digital form. It received accolades across the operations and was a showpiece for the department.

Imagine if I did not have an intentional plan to complete my MBA and the vision board, and if I was not disciplined nor consistent, and I allowed distractions to interfere and derail me. Nothing would have been achieved. This story is about trying to complete my MBA and developing a vision board while working at a very demanding job, but it can be applied to all areas of life that you desire to change.

v. Key Reflections

Intentional living requires you to declutter your mind, just like your wardrobes need tidying up and you must schedule time to do this. Living intentionally is living by design and helps you to become self-aware having developed a clear plan.

First class performance requires the following considerations.

- Be deliberate
- Create quiet moments to reflect and envision
- Be disciplined and set goals
- Embrace imperfections
- Be consistent
- Keep track, monitor progress, and seek feedback.

CHAPTER 4
BE AUTHENTIC

To be authentic requires you to act in ways that show your true self and how you feel. Express yourself genuinely and don't be afraid to be yourself. Showing people only one side of you is a disservice to the world. The world needs all of you with all the greatness you carry. Releasing yourself to be yourself, will enable you to connect with others genuinely and add value to them while being fulfilled. The journey to being authentic starts with knowing yourself. In the process of identifying and showing your authenticity, your uniqueness will be birthed. It is important to note that time and energy are required to find and develop your uniqueness

i. Know Yourself

Knowing yourself is a key step to being authentic. To know yourself, you need to recognize different parts of your identity and personality, with a goal to acknowledge all you are. You need to be open to learning new things about yourself. This takes us to the next stage, which is being self-aware.

Be Self-aware: To be self-aware, you need to be aware of your strengths and weaknesses. You need to know your capabilities and evaluate where there are shortcomings. You need to know what makes you happy or not. This knowledge will shape your thoughts and actions, guiding where and how you spend your time, and on which activities and goals, enabling you to be productive. Some key questions to help you understand yourself are: what do you love doing and what legacy do you want to leave?

Be Mindful: Being mindful is another key element in knowing yourself. This was discussed in chapters 1 and 3 extensively. It means experiencing the present moment to understand your thoughts and actions. You need to pay attention to yourself, and the world as you see and experience it. Daily mindful habits include, taking a few minutes to pause and observe the world around you. This helps you better understand yourself and why you take actions or why you do not.

Self-acceptance: On this journey, you must be ready for self-acceptance, that is, to accept your weak points and leverage your strong points. There is no perfect person, therefore you need to be ready to accept your weak points and leverage the strength of others. The fact that you are not good at a particular subject or area does not mean you cannot seek knowledge from others to improve that area.

In life, we will always function within a team, in the family or workplace. To function effectively within a team, you need to be self-aware and ready to accept yourself as you are. Being authentic will help you focus your energy on your strengths, be true to yourself, and act without fear of being caught pretending to be someone you are not.

As individuals, we are constantly learning and we can always leverage on each other for knowledge sharing. Through knowledge share initiative, a program where people are assigned to research and share knowledge on different topics. I have been able to learn about different areas of business or life from others. This was done across my secondary school alumni where mates are scheduled to lead different topics which cuts across life – career, health, family, entrepreneurship etc. We had a schedule for the topics to accommodate all members. This enabled people to stretch and take topics that were not really their area of specialty. I have also seen this model work well within a workplace where it was used to disrupt and ensure employees do not remain within their comfort zone. It disrupted learning experiences and enabled people to acknowledge their areas of improvement and leverage on others depending on their strengths.

ii. Be Yourself

Having decided to live intentionally and to begin to get to know yourself, the next step is to be yourself. Live your life how you want to live it regardless of the opinions of other people. To be authentic, you need to be yourself and let people see you for who you are.

Evaluate Doubts: As you progress in life, you will have doubts or feelings of inadequacy. You will doubt your ability to perform some duties, which is what is referred to as imposter syndrome. Everyone feels this way at one time or the other, but it is important to ensure that you deal with imposter syndrome promptly.

One way of dealing with imposter syndrome is to remind yourself about your past achievements, which is the foundation that propels you to aim higher and do more. You can also look at yourself in the mirror and talk to yourself about your past achievements. To deal with your doubts, you need to focus on your strengths. Once, I applied for a senior role and was shortlisted as one of the qualified candidates. Then, I was scheduled for an interview. However, because of imposter syndrome, I declined the interview by making excuses that I could have worked around if I had believed more in myself. I allowed my doubts to overshadow my capabilities and strengths.

I have learned over the years to take appropriate steps to address imposter syndrome whenever it occurs. A few years ago, I was designated to lead a new technology awareness campaign across the organization. This was within a large organization. I was also scheduled to lead a team to one of our stakeholders. The feeling of inadequacy returned. I wondered if I was qualified enough to communicate the concept, I wondered if the audience would believe me, I wondered how I would look if it didn't resonate well with the audience. However, I reflected on my past successes, which gave me courage as I took on the challenge. Then I researched, studied, and practiced my presentation.

With a greater measure of confidence, we (I led my team) to the other departments. Through the campaign we were able to get people stirred up on the need for change and by the time we completed the project, I was applauded for doing a great job. That singular activity enabled me to realize that I had more capabilities than I thought I had. I discovered that I could speak passionately and move people to be committed to a cause. I would not have been aware of all these, if I had succumbed to imposter syndrome and not accepted the challenge to lead my team on the campaign.

Develop Courage: You will have fears and doubts. However, taking steps even in the midst of fear is what will differentiate you and shift you from your comfort zone. You cannot make an impact from your comfort zone. I was scheduled to research an agreed industry specific topic and present an output to an executive committee. This was another cap on a busy schedule with little time for attention. I was not deliberate in creating time to prepare and until the day before the presentation. My fears kicked in with feelings of inadequacy, I engaged to seek opportunity to change the date which met a brick wall. Since the day was fixed, I had to summon courage to prepare even within a short time. With the research materials, I prepared my slides and conducted the knowledge share session. It was very well received and led to many other sessions to disseminate the same information across different cadres within the organization.

Through this experience, I learnt that I could grow in any situation, even those that are not within my comfort zone. Some of the skills I picked up during that time are what I use effectively today.

Living Your Values: Living your values is critical to showing your authentic self. The values you communicate determine how people view your authenticity. What are your values and how do you live them out through your daily activities? Do you communicate your values through your actions? Your interactions at home, in the office, and during any engagement must be consistent and must reflect your values. Delivering tasks with excellence and ensuring that you add value to any task, are examples of living your values.

Love Yourself: Learn to love yourself and think good thoughts about yourself. This propels you forward because you can be rest assured that you are good enough while you are still evolving. Understanding that feedback is a blessing is instrumental to loving yourself because people will give you feedback based on their experience of you. When you have good thoughts about yourself, negative feedback will not affect you adversely. Rather, it will propel you to identify improvement opportunities and close any identified gaps. Try this exercise, write ten things you love about yourself. If you can write ten, increase it to 100 by progressing in multiples of ten. You will be amazed at how your confidence will grow with the associated ripple effect on your total transformation. Loving yourself is key to being authentic. It helps to free you of the worry of how you come across to others.

iii. Improve Yourself

Improving yourself is a continuous exercise that is critical to your authenticity. It can be expressed in different ways, for example, reading a book daily, or learning a new skill or a new language. You can also attend seminars and conferences. With evolving technology, there are no barriers to self-improvement as most improvement plans can be done virtually. The internet ensures that we do not have to be physically present at different locations in our quest for self-improvement.

Growth Mindset: Having a growth mindset set is the foundation for improving yourself. A growth mindset as elaborated in chapter 1 is a willingness to learn new things, understanding that the world is not perfect and no one is, and knowing that failures and mistakes are learning opportunities. You can learn new things in your personal life or your career, by seeking out how other professionals have charted a path you are about to venture into.

Recently I registered for a technology industry virtual summit to engage with other professionals who had the same or a higher level of experience than I had. It was an opportunity to learn from them and understand how things work in advanced markets while networking. The summit opened me up to opportunities to learn new things, further validate the things I was already working on, and see opportunities to localize or optimize our processes based on my new insights. An individual with a growth mindset has to constantly seek knowledge, learn new things, and be willing to seek help from others. Failures and mistakes are inevitable and will help you grow and develop.

Remember the interview for the senior role that I declined? Even though that was a mistake on my part, I learnt some lessons from that experience. Two major learning points were to believe more in myself and trust myself more, which have been very helpful. Trust yourself, build self-confidence, and allow others to trust you more. This is further reinforced through self-love and a growth mindset.

Follow Your Intuition: By following your intuition, you open your mind to trust your thoughts and feelings. Trust your guts, especially when you have to make quick decisions. Once, I had a spontaneous thought to write a post on social media specifically Facebook & Instagram about making bold moves despite fear. The feedback from the post showed that many lives were touched. What I shared helped some people overcome fear and make progress on their examinations with success. Many ideas come to your mind, which you can use to improve yourself or others. Learn to trust yourself and know that you will get better with time.

iv. Discover Purpose

You can discover purpose by being authentic. Your purpose is the reason for your existence, which might be bigger than yourself or those around you and will occur over time.

I received feedback from a junior colleague, two years after I left the multinational organization that I had imparted knowledge to him by my actions. A project update was required by senior management which he provided while I was present at the session. Unknowingly, there was an error in the details provided. Realizing his error, he informed me about it, since I was leading the transformation. So, I went back to the head of department to correct the initial wrong submission. He stated that he was shocked that I could open up about an incorrectly submitted information considering the pressured timelines and the need to deliver immediate value. The update will stretch the timelines a bit but it was a better position to hold back and negatively impact the business expectations. I did not see anything unusual in my actions because I wanted the head of the department to have the right update for his next meeting, considering it was a high-visibility project. My former colleague informed me that this scenario taught him career and leadership lessons about taking ownership without giving excuses, knowing your boss, and knowing how to relate with your boss.

I did not realize I was modeling these lessons, which others have attested to, over the years. That incident was an unknown opportunity that transformed someone's life. As we progress in life, we model many lessons to others just by being our authentic selves. Your authenticity will enable you to realize your potential because it will help you achieve impossible feats while transforming people's lives along your journey. When you know yourself, be yourself, live your values, and love your life, you will discover purpose and realize your potential.

Part of being authentic is being vulnerable and admitting to mistakes. There is nothing wrong with this, especially if you are learning from your mistakes which are missed opportunities. By being vulnerable, you develop the courage to be yourself irrespective of what others say.

Discovering your purpose is a journey, which can be long-term. You become comfortable with being authentic as you develop and grow. You need to learn to exercise patience as you navigate your journey.

v. Key Reflections

You must be ready to invest that time by addressing key points like being self-aware, being mindful, with readiness to accept yourself as you are. Important considerations to being authentic are

- Know Yourself and Trust Your Capabilities
- Be Yourself
- Improve Yourself
- Discover Purpose

CHAPTER 5
STAY POSITIVE AND BE GRATEFUL

There is always something to be grateful for, no matter the season. Cultivate the habit of gratitude and watch your life transform. Gratitude changes everything. Do you appreciate where you are, on the way to where you are going? Are you fixed on what is happening on the other side that looks brighter? Do not fret! Make the best of whatever you have and be thankful for your current state. Every experience is preparation for the future. Shift your focus to gratitude. By being grateful, you remain positive and can hope for the best. An optimistic view of life will always see the good in everything.

i. Your Thoughts Matter

What you think about will gradually manifest. If you constantly dwell on negative thoughts, you will always expect negative things to happen and this does not add any value to you. How do you change your negative thoughts to positive thoughts? It is critical to have an optimistic viewpoint in all circumstances, and this requires deliberate effort. When you notice your thoughts going in the wrong direction, stop, take a deep breath, and refocus.

Positivity and Focus: Starting your day with positivity is another way to ensure positive engaging thoughts, which has a way of determining the outlook of the day. Why worry about things outside your control as you go about your day? While I understand that this cannot be totally eradicated, it is more important to focus your energy on things within your control. I recall the early days in my career when there was no career growth due to the nature of the organization. Imagine being in one position for many years. There was a tendency to start worrying about how to change the structure, this was not within my control and I could not change this. I chose to rather focus my energy on developing myself for other opportunities. I led major projects which stretched me to read wide, engage with multiple stakeholders and have deep knowledge about other business areas. I gained experience on the current role and remained positive. Although the other opportunities were not fully ready and available, the preparation which was within my control got my attention. This got me busy and focused.

ii. Cultivate an Attitude of Gratitude

There is always something to be grateful for. Gratitude has to become a conscious habit. This forces you to re-channel your energy to the big picture rather than focusing on challenges and problems. Do you have a gratitude list or journal? Keeping a gratitude journal will help you quantify and appreciate the great things happening in your life. No matter how small, there is always something to be thankful for. Be thankful about the little things and gradually the big things will appear. Keep a gratitude journal that is focused on family, health, career, or any other area of life.

Gratitude Journal: Your gratitude could be journaled daily, weekly, or monthly. I have a friend who is constantly posting on social media, her thankful series, which is focused on even the little things of life. One week, she is thankful for the fruits in season and the benefits they provide to the body, another week she is thankful for being stuck in traffic recognizing the fact that Lagos is traffic prone while yet another week, she is thankful for the opportunity to wake up in good health. She has even written about her name and how thankful she is to have that name, sharing its meaning and how it has impacted her life. While reflecting in your journal, you will appreciate your progress and indeed realize that you are blessed. You also need to decide where to journal. This can be in paper form or electronic form. There are also available applications on the phone for journaling. Decide on whichever suits you as an individual and remain consistent with it. Overall, there is always a reason to be thankful.

Celebrate your wins: Celebrating your wins, both the little and big wins, helps cultivate a grateful attitude. When you celebrate you release some feel-good energy called endorphins into your body, and this fuels you to achieve more. Rewarding yourself with a drink, a visit to the spa, or movie time with family are some simple ways to celebrate your wins. Staying grateful helps you maintain a positive attitude to life.

iii. Your Environment and its Impact

Make sure your environment is structured to generate positive feelings. Having too much negativity surrounding you is not a good thing. Is your environment conducive enough? A positive environment increases positive emotions and wellbeing. Surround yourself with positive people. Remember the saying, birds of the same feather flock together. Whoever you hang out with rubs off on you. If you are surrounded by negative-minded individuals, then your view will always be negative. I have heard about instances where serious-minded people began associating with people with a negative mindset and this affected their performance and overall outlook unfavorably. When you surround yourself with positive people, you will hear positive stories and have a positive outlook, which will affect your thinking, words, and actions. You must also bring positivity to others.

"When a flower does not bloom, you fix the environment in which it grows, not the flower"
-Alexander Den Heijer

To flourish in life, you have to be deliberate about your environment.

You need to be alert regarding life issues that can have a negative impact on you. For example, combining family and a career can be stressful for females, especially if they have hectic schedules. Trying to have a baby for years and exploring multiple fertility options can impact your mood negatively. Remaining stagnant in a role for five years with no promotion in sight can also take a toll on your attitude. These are environmental factors that we cannot control so it is better to focus on things that are within our control. We can deliberately surround ourselves with positive and grateful people who rub off on us while we are waiting for change.

Who is around you? How are they influencing your thoughts? Where do you visit? You can choose to go where you will be celebrated.

iv. Add Value to Others

Staying Positive allows you to add value to other people because you can listen to them and help them. Many years ago, there was a particular senior colleague, anytime she came into the office, she would go round all team members wishing them good morning, asking about their family and just generally have a small talk to engage and build rapport with the team. She spends about a minute or 2mins by each team member's desk. Her actions were very effective in building positivity and boosting morale. Employees felt that they are not just a number in the business and that their contribution and welfare matters. This enabled the team to generate positive energy with a readiness to go the extra mile.

I have committed to doing the same over the years, and the result has been tremendous to myself and others that I interact with. I say good morning to everyone irrespective of their level within the organization. I make small talk to find out how they and their family are doing. I use the opportunity to find out the names of their family members and the next time I say hello, I can ask about their children, even mentioning their names. This lifts the mood of the individual and I feel fulfilled every time I see their response, which is a smile. Overall, these actions boost morale.

As a senior manager with managers and engineers within my team, I recall one of the engineers approached me stating he had received a query from his manager. They were both members of my team. He approached me to guide on the best approach to respond and address the query. Initially, I felt a bit offended that I was being consulted on how to respond to the query. The query emanated from my direct report, his manager to the engineer, and I the senior manager was being consulted on how to respond. On second thoughts and proper reflection, I realized it was because of the mode of engagement, he felt he could easily relate with me to evaluate and chart way forward. By demonstrating that I was ready to listen, it opened a channel of engagement for value addition.

Listening and Helping Others: To stay positive and grateful, there is a need to listen to and help others. This is another way of adding value. This could be in the form of coaching for performance. Through this coaching, an individual is able to discover gaps for improvement. By adding value to people, you will see them beginning to bloom and there is a feeling of fulfilment. Within four years, seven team members who were reporting to me were promoted to managerial roles. This is an achievement for them during their career journey. They were coached at different stages, provided with opportunities to challenge themselves and lead value adding deliveries. There were occasions they represented me in meetings. These exposure and experiences shaped them to become better and more knowledgeable. They were able to showcase their diligence during this engagement. When opportunities opened up and they were prepared for the higher positions and performed well during the interviews. They were committed to their success and took up responsibility to continuously evolve. Some of these new promotions even took some of them out of the technology division. It was fulfilling to be part of their success and see them evolve and transform. Staying positive and being grateful shifts your focus from negativity to adding value. It puts you in a position to think differently.

v. Key Reflections

Staying Positive and Grateful is a deliberate effort to maintain your peace and flourish irrespective of what is happening around you. Do this by practicing these steps.

- Watch your thoughts
- Cultivate gratitude attitude
- Learn to journal
- Be ready to add value to others

CHAPTER 6
SEEK KNOWLEDGE

You need to actively seek knowledge to increase power. According to Alvin Toffler, "The illiterate of the 21st century will not be those who cannot read and write, but those who cannot learn, unlearn, and relearn." As you learn, you need to apply the knowledge you've acquired. This is a continuous exercise that requires the right attitude to achieve success. In this global and rapidly evolving landscape, knowledge is the new currency, therefore a thirst for knowledge is crucial. Knowledge economy allows the use of knowledge in creating products and services, providing new sources of economic growth and high productivity. Personal development is an important lifelong process to fully maximize your potential. Seeking and sharing knowledge requires consistent, deliberate, and conscious effort. In the past, you had to be physically present in a classroom for formal training, but technology has eliminated the location barrier and learning can occur without borders, today. The ability to learn is key to success and growth in your career. Individuals need to have knowledge, and continuously improve and grow their skills to stay ahead of the pack.

i. Cultivate a Learning Mindset

A key element for an evolving mind in an evolving world is a learning mindset. The tools and techniques you knew in the past are fast becoming irrelevant for today's use because we   face complex challenges that require a problem-solving mindset. Without a learning mindset, you will be stuck with the old ways of doing things. The course you studied at university will not fully meet the knowledge or work experience required for your future job. You need to learn new skills because your environment keeps changing. Technology, for example, is constantly evolving and we are now discussing the Fourth Industrial Revolution. A mindset that remained stuck on the First Industrial Revolution, could not have survived the Second or Third Industrial Revolution.

A learning mindset will consistently seek opportunities to learn new things, new ways of doing things, and new skills. A learning mindset means that you are adaptable as the times change. The fact that you studied physics in the university does not mean you will become a teacher. I have seen … people with degrees in agriculture become technology providers. People with science-oriented degrees have become business and commercial minded professionals, who are driving business strategy and transformation. There is no limit, and you can evolve to become who you want as long as you have the right mindset, chart a roadmap, and are ready to remain committed to achieving your plan.

Problem-solving: Problem-solving is a key attribute of individuals who are always willing to explore ways to address problems and challenges they encounter on the way. There has been evolution over the years and most discussions or initiatives now occur using the internet for discovery and delivery. People are adapting to this new normal. If you do not adapt to changes in line with the trends in your industry, you could become not only disadvantaged but also extinct because you will not be able to add value or contribute effectively.

Adopting Your Hobbies: You can improve your mindset by exploring new hobbies or developing old ones. New hobbies can include things that you wanted to learn or explore as a child. Learning new hobbies or exploring old ones can be exciting, and it helps with improving your skills so you can grow and evolve.

Conduct a Skills Audit: You can conduct a skills audit to put together your personal development plan. You don't have to wait for an organization to train you. Whatever you learn is yours, no one will take it from you. Instead, what you learn will transform you and give you more experience. Most times, people lament that organizations do not train them. While it is good to receive valuable training from your organization, depending on your organization to train you, especially when it is not forthcoming, is allowing your future to waste. A focused individual needs to cultivate a learning mindset, constantly coming up with solutions to drive increased productivity irrespective of where he or she finds him or herself.

You can reinvent yourself through continuous personal development. Commit to your personal development; be adaptable and ready to make changes to be a lifelong learner. I conducted a skills audit about six years ago and based on the output, I created a growth and development plan. Over the years, this growth plan took a back seat because of many distractions, and I was negligent in consistently tracking the plan. Recently, I revisited the plan and I was excited to discover that I had achieved quite a number of my goals, which revolved around reinvention and continuous development. Recently, I joined multiple virtual summits to discuss technology and its impact amongst global industry players. A thirst for knowledge and insight regarding other markets led me to register for and attend the summits. It was quite insightful to learn that industry players had similar challenges, irrespective of geographical location.

Be Adaptable: To be a learner, you must be adaptable. Being adaptable is the ability to respond quickly to changes within an environment. It involves constantly evolving ideas, trends, and responsibilities or strategies. Adaptability helps you deal with adversities and challenges should they occur. This further increases your chances to succeed. For example, the COVID-19 pandemic was a disruption that required everyone to be adaptable in order to survive the season.

Be a Lifelong Learner: As a lifelong learner, you need to be self-motivated in the pursuit of knowledge. This applies to not only your professional life but also your personal life. Learnings can occur daily, knowingly and unknowingly. You can unknowingly learn new things through your interactions with people and projects. However, the major push is to be deliberate and seek knowledge, especially in areas where you are deficient. An individual can identify areas of development annually and work out a plan to address it. This plan can become the goal for a new year. To stay relevant, there is a need to keep learning.

ii. Create Time

As a lifelong learner, you need to consciously create or schedule time for learning. It may be once a day or a weekly learning schedule. It could be first thing in the morning or last thing at night. At some point during my career, some of my colleagues would always come in before 8 a.m. to study our vendor's documents so that they could be well informed about different solutions. What then happened was that they became like experts because other team members would always ask the early risers for solutions to challenges. To be productive, especially if you are considering having some quiet time without distractions, you can start your daily learning session by 5 a.m. when others are still asleep.

Define Your Learning Goals: Learning goals need to be defined, as this will guide your outcomes. What do you need additional knowledge about? Your career, industry, family, parenting, marriage, sports, or faith? Once you have identified the area(s), you can build your themes into your development plan. You also need to consider a focus area at any given time. This applies if you are considering multiple themes. For example, you can focus on career improvement in the morning and on parenting, mid-week. How often will you have to read, once a week or twice a week?

Be Consistent: Being consistent with whatever pattern you chose is key to achieving results. If you miss one of your planned goals, do not give up, continue with your learning goals. There is no need to worry unnecessarily. Learn from the missed goal, identify what you need to do differently, and continue your learning journey. An accountability partner can act as a great support system. Your accountability partner could be a colleague, friend, or anyone who can hold you accountable and ensure you follow through with your plan. Accountability can also take the form of a mention to your friend that you plan to wake up at 5 a.m. every day to catch up on industry knowledge as a way to stay ahead of the game in your career. Every time your friend sees you, they will ask you if you followed through with your commitment. That is a way of ensuring that you focus on your goal and achieve the desired value.

iii. Acknowledge Ignorance and Know it is Short-lived

Be comfortable with ignorance but not for too long. It is okay not to know everything, but the onus is on you to take action to obtain knowledge. The first step is to acknowledge your ignorance because no one knows it all. If you are in a meeting, and you are asked a question for which you do not have the answer, there is nothing wrong in saying, "I will check and provide feedback." What is important is to ensure that you get the required information and provide feedback as you committed to do. Avoid making this a pattern. Once you understand the theme or agenda of meetings, you can prepare in advance to avoid having to consistently get back with updates and responses to issues raised during meetings.

Recall the experience that I shared earlier of being a young graduate who was understudying a senior colleague? We were posted to a multinational organization and within two weeks of resumption, the senior colleague resigned. I was left alone to support critical systems and provide quality service to the organization. It was quite challenging at the beginning, however I assumed responsibility for the delivery and started seeking additional knowledge. I even joined blogs online to learn about and understand the challenges that other system engineers had encountered while delivering similar services. I was forced to grow on the job because I had to spend plenty of time learning while solving the issues that came up. By the time I was leaving the organization about two years later, I received a Gold Commendation. The organization requested that my replacement be as experienced as I was.

You need to learn to ask questions if you require clarity. Be comfortable with not knowing, but only for a short while and take appropriate steps to learn. It is equally good to ask for help from a coach, mentor, friend, or colleague, if you require support. You are only ignorant for a moment. You will become wiser in that area as soon as you take appropriate steps to obtain knowledge. While asking for help, you will get both positive and negative responses. Be tough-skinned enough to accept the negative responses without bad feelings. Learn from each experience and move on.

Share Knowledge to Improve Confidence: Sharing knowledge is another way to grow what you already know by sharing ideas, thoughts or industry knowledge with people. What do you know that others do not know? One way to deepen your knowledge is to share that knowledge with others. By sharing knowledge, you will gain insights from others. Recall the time when I was assigned to present and share knowledge to an executive team? Out of fear and lack of discipline, I did not take it seriously and was busy carrying out my normal job functions until a day before the meeting. I requested for a change in date, but it was declined. I had to summon courage and study diligently, staying up late into the night. The next morning, after I made the presentation, the feedback was very impressive.

By sharing knowledge, I became more informed about the topic of discussion and I was able to share the same knowledge to the entire department on another occasion. I gained new insights by studying the topic and thinking through how it can be applied within the organization because I had to educate others. Other people's perspectives changed my view. The questions, comments, and feedback from the audience also highlighted new learnings for me and positioned me as a subject-matter expert. The knowledge sharing experience also exposed me to new possibilities because that experience helped me grow. Application of the knowledge I gained to my work reshaped the way I engaged with stakeholders and partners, creating possibilities for collaboration in the future. By experiencing fear and overcoming it, you will develop a thick skin and greater confidence to share your knowledge, impacting lives in the process.

Knowledge sharing is the exchange of knowledge among people, friends, and families, within and outside an organization. While the example above occurred within a professional setting, knowledge sharing can occur within community-based organizations and can be applied anywhere. Knowledge can be shared in meetings and virtual sessions using collaboration tools such as videos and other channels. Knowledge share is a great leadership trait. By actively modelling knowledge share, you showcase the need for open and timely idea and information exchange among team members. This will lead to reciprocity because others will be willing to share their knowledge too, seeing it as an opportunity to impact lives and add value to others.

iv. Key Reflections

To remain relevant, you need to be ready to learn and develop a desire to grow. Learning is a continuous journey and requires flexibility as you progress. You can seek an accountability partner if you are struggling to keep up with your development plan. Important and basic considerations required to evolve and transform to a lifelong learner are listed

- Cultivating a learning mindset prepares you to be adaptable and ready to seek new ways of doing things.

A learning mindset means that you are adaptable as the times change.

- You need to deliberately create time, define your goals and be consistent
- Acknowledge ignorance and know it is short-lived on the journey to improve your confidence

CHAPTER 7
UNCOVER TRUE POTENTIAL

There is so much more in you than you realize. Most times, you do not know the capabilities that exist within you. These unknown capabilities are potential, they are necessary abilities that can be used to become successful in the future. True potential is hidden, waiting to be exploited. Learn to express your gift because someone needs that unique gift of yours. Learn to express it although you may think that everyone already knows what you want to share, so what is the use? Don't give up on a great idea. Your unique personality and experiences make up a unique you and therefore a unique gift.

i. True Potential is Hidden

You need to discover your potential, use it, and nurture it while giving yourself an opportunity to shine. Discovering your potential requires effort on your part. After you discover your potential, you can proceed to use and nurture it through various means, which will be discussed as we go along.

Human beings are full of unrealized capabilities. Recall the example I shared in chapter 2 where I had set up a WhatsApp group for my secondary school alumni to reunite classmates about twenty-two years after we graduated. I proceeded to do this, and the group now hosts close to 200 classmates spread across the world. The journey has been very enlightening with loads of opportunities to discover new capabilities I did not realize I possessed because I assumed responsibilities within the group. I discovered some of my hidden potential and was able to use it effectively to add value. Through this platform, many other classmates have discovered new talents that they are using as a means of livelihood. Within the alumni group, I was able to develop a newsletter and lead other knowledge-sharing initiatives, some of which I would not have embarked on if I were not on the alumni platform. I have also used some of the hidden skills I discovered while assuming responsibilities on the alumni whatsapp group in other spheres of life like marriage, career, and relationships. You cannot afford to rest on your past successes. Therefore, it is important to take steps to uncover your true potential, as we shall see as we go along.

Nurture Your Potential: Nurturing your potential requires you to stretch yourself and give of yourself. Step out of your comfort zone and expand your boundaries. To achieve extraordinary things, you have to be extraordinary, which includes fully using all the potential you have. Being on this journey of nurturing your potential can be empowering and fulfilling as you discover new talents in different areas of life and business.

ii. Be Self-aware

The first step to uncovering your hidden potential is becoming self-aware. Understand your feelings as an individual and discover the talents that exist within you. Talent can be discovered through peer and team development, coaching, and teaching. Through the experience of forming a WhatsApp group of about 200 alumni members drawn from across the world, I developed key skills around organizing and ideation. Assuming responsibilities on the group provided opportunities to develop solutions for issues or challenges that we encountered. Feedback from other members of the group indicated that they had been inspired to become more than they were. Feedback is a blessing and can be used as an avenue to become self-aware. People, including, professional associates, friends, and family will provide you with solicited and unsolicited feedback. This feedback will further sharpen your awareness of yourself and your capabilities. I received feedback from alumni members about capabilities that I never knew I possessed or did not regard as valuable. You might not find immediate use for some of the capabilities discovered, however it is important to formulate a plan to start using your newly discovered capability.

A friend of mine received feedback on an ongoing anniversary planning project that helped him discover his ability to engage an audience constructively in a relaxed atmosphere. He received the feedback in good faith but he could not exploit his new capabilities until 3 months later, when an opportunity to work on an annual review project came his way. This project had a bigger platform and came with countless challenges, but he was able to effectively deploy his public speaking skills. His performance brought him visibility and created an opportunity for him to shine within and outside his normal sphere of influence. He now actively speaks and anchors events across industries.

iii. Volunteering

Volunteering in your organization, community, and alumni associations are ways to use your potential once it has been identified. I know someone who served as a security guard in a church. He later joined a church group and gradually discovered his talent for photography, which he has developed and converted into a full-fledged business that generates his only source of income. Volunteering provides opportunities to stretch you beyond your core functions and duties. Tunde, a friend of mine has through volunteering and supporting the financial management of his alumni association has learnt new skills on how to better present data to non-finance professionals, he reports finances in pictures with good visuals for everyone to understand. He has been applying these new skills within his workplace and it has brought him recognition from his senior management team.

iv. Challenging Projects and Experiences

Challenges are also another way to discover true potential. Life experiences and tough situations can help us discover unused potential. For instance, someone who is experiencing financial challenges may have to be creative as he or she explores opportunities to generate new income or produce results at cheaper costs. Your core job function might not involve project management, however getting involved in projects and volunteering to take up responsibilities can expose you to various hidden capabilities, which can be further exploited. There have been many cases where major successes are recorded from this. Often, we go through these challenging experiences and become tough skinned in the process. The learnings from these experiences and projects remain with the individual. These learnings become a foundation for subsequent wins.

v. Key Reflections

There is a lot of potential in us waiting to be unleashed and exploited. To do this effectively, you need to engage these reflections

- Be ready to stretch beyond your comfort zone and push boundaries
- As you discover your hidden talent and capabilities, create a plan to nurture them
- Become self aware of these capabilities
- You can seek opportunities to uncover your hidden potentials through volunteering, challenging projects and experiences

CHAPTER 8
CULTIVATE RELATIONSHIPS

Relationships are vital to success because no man is an island. People do business with people they know, like, and trust. Trust is an essential attribute that can only be developed through relationships. We meet all kinds of people at different stages in our lives and careers, and we need to ensure that these engagements become fruitful relationships. To influence people, you need to focus on relationships and ensure that your relationships add value. Cultivating relationships puts us in a better light as we progress in life.

i. Connect With People

You need to make a deliberate effort to connect with people, and you can do this in many ways, like smiling at the next person, initiating conversations, or offering compliments. Whichever way you choose, you need to stay connected with people.

Show Empathy: Empathy is the capacity to understand what another person is experiencing or to see things from their perspective. This is different from sympathy. Sympathy refers to feeling sad about someone's misfortune while empathy allows you to connect and help them. Empathy is not about feeling sad or pity for people, it is about feeling and hearing people. We like to feel heard and understood. By empathizing with others, you show understanding of their feelings, and you can communicate your understanding of their feelings effectively, seeing the world as they see it.

Empathy can be used within or outside an organization, applied to family, the home, your career, business, and life in general. We constantly relate with others, and it is important to show empathy. Let others see that you are interested in them and can empathize with them, by seeing things from their frame of reference. This can only happen by engaging others and building relationships, which can bloom into showing empathy. Being deliberate about saying good morning to your colleagues and asking how they and their family are, irrespective of their experience or position, can open you up to having better relationships with them. Most times, we receive a smile in return while our colleagues are responding. This creates an avenue to continue making small talk, which can evolve into more engaging discussions. By recognizing someone in pain, you are better able to support them.

We can also extend empathy to ourselves and accept our emotions. This will flow into how we engage and interact with others. Once we establish relationships, managing them requires tact and focus. I remember seeing someone who is usually bubbly, somewhat downcast. I said good morning to him and asked how he was doing. Then I commented that he seemed to be a bit dull. He appreciated the fact that someone had noticed his mood change and that energized him to brighten up. This underscores the need to take a genuine interest in people.

Develop Genuine Interest in People: Having a genuine interest in people is a great way to start relationships. How much interest do you show in people? Being empathetic means that you see things from other people's perspective, which implies that you are genuinely interested in them. Find commonalities through discussions with others. To show interest in people, some key questions to ask include, are they growing, do they need support, and are they making mistakes? If you are genuinely interested, you will be able to provide support. Your interest in people can also be shown by your gestures and actions, through talking and communicating, or even the way you address people. You cannot state that you are genuinely interested in someone and not call his or her attention, however subtly, to a wrong step or mistake. You can offer support to close any improvement gaps or highlight progress.

Appreciate People: Show appreciation when you receive value, even in little things. Nothing is so small that you cannot say thank you for. When you appreciate the little things, the big things will come along. It is important to appreciate yourself and your progress no matter how small, and to extend this kind of appreciation to others. Recognizing the good qualities of a person has an exponential effect. People do more for those who appreciate them. Always seek opportunities to appreciate people, and to acknowledge progress and results. Develop the courage to celebrate people because this also speaks a lot about how aware you are, and you do not need to feel intimidated or less valued in the process. Valuing others reflects positively on you. Some ways to show appreciation include, saying thank you, using various collaboration platforms, taking someone out to lunch, or calling them just to share your appreciation. Within organizations, platforms are created to shine the light on employees as a form of appreciation and some these include giving of awards. Platforms like LinkedIn have a Kudos feature to acknowledge the contributions of connections or celebrate their achievements. One of my senior colleagues celebrated me on LinkedIn and it made me feel good and valued. It also served as a form of validation to showcase my value to others.

There is value in showing that you recognize and enjoy the good qualities in someone because most times, the person is not aware of their good qualities. By celebrating people, they become more aware of their strong qualities and are motivated to develop them. Showing empathy, having a genuine interest in people, and appreciating them, are great ways to connect with people.

ii. Be Ready to Influence People

Influence is developed through relationships. Think about the people who have influenced you. They were able to do so through relationships and trust. You will be influenced by people, when you believe in them. Cultivating relationships for influence requires you to make connections and build interactions which requires time and energy. To start influencing people, you need to evaluate your associations. This is a critical step in the process.

Your Association Matters: Who do you associate with and why do you associate with them? What value do you derive from your associations? What is the aim of each of your relationships? Relationships need to have defined goals because your goals will guide how you build and nurture your relationships. Is a relationship geared to bring out the best in you, to compliment you, or to open you up to growth or networking opportunities? We all need encouragers and those who lift us up in our lives, not discouragers.

On the journey of life, some long-standing associations are still valuable today while others have fallen away. I have some friendships that are fourteen years' old. Although these friends and I have evolved over the years, we have remained in touch and supportive of one another, as the need arises. In the early days of my career, I had a senior colleague whom I could always reach out to whenever I needed financial assistance. I also played my part in the relationship by ensuring that I paid back the loan. I still maintain a good relationship with him today and our families are now quite close. Some of my associations have become my support system. For example, when I need to attend an event or meeting, I drop off my kids with them. I share experiences and brainstorm ideas with them, and others are now sponsors of my various initiatives. We constantly influence each other.

iii. Nurture Relationships

Imagine if I did not nurture my relationships or had differences that were not settled. Relationships must be nurtured carefully by both parties, providing value to each other for a mutually beneficial connection.

Settle Differences: We will always have differences of opinions, ideas, or in our preferences, but the onus is on us to always find creative ways to resolve our disputes or conflicts. Having crucial conversations involves dealing with difficult issues to chart a resolution. Empathy plays a part in having these conversations.

A friend had a conflict with her immediate boss over work delivery. Neither party was willing to budge as each felt strongly about their position on the matter. The issue escalated, necessitating intervention by another executive. Eventually the matter was closed through multiple engagements. However, the resolution was not fully discussed, and this put a strain on the relationship, although both parties tried not to negatively impact work further. In my opinion, the issue could have been treated differently and even the way it was escalated, should have been handled in a matured way. I also think that my friend should have apologized to her boss, however she was not willing to.

Fast forward seven months later, and I found myself facing an interview panel for a senior role with another entity, and my friend's boss was one of the panelists. The score for the interview was not only based on the evaluation during the interview but also past job performance and attitude. What if my friend was the interviewee facing the panel, I thought? I felt certain that the ugly experience she had had with her boss would have affected her performance negatively.

I have also seen instances where former colleagues who you assumed were irrelevant, now become relevant when they suddenly occupy positions that can be beneficial to you. Therefore, it is important to settle differences by having crucial conversations. These crucial conversations will require a discussion on the conflicting views and together the involved parties will chart a way to address and minimize frictions.

Don't Burn Bridges: We build bridges through relationships, and it is vital not to burn these bridges. At a summit I attended last year, I met all my previous senior colleagues. We were all attending the same event as executives because we were all now on the same level. Who could have imagined this five or six years ago? It was a humbling experience. A colleague who was a manager, left our multinational technology organization for a role in a newly formed organization within the same industry. He returned to work for the multinational technology organization five years later as a senior manager, which is a more senior role. Imagine if he had burnt bridges, or not handled the relationships developed well. He would not have considered applying for the role or he might not have been shortlisted for the senior manager interview. There is another colleague who resigned and during his last months within the organization, his relationship with colleagues was almost strained due to concerns he had around the exit process; thankfully this was addressed before his final exit. Within 6 months of leaving the organization, he needed references, support and knowledge on areas of low competency. He had to connect with his former colleagues. Imagine if all these people have strained relationships with their colleagues, further engagement would not have been possible, and opportunities will be lost.

Adopt a Win-Win Model That is Mutually Beneficial: A win-win model needs to be adopted in nurturing relationships, so all parties benefit one way or another. All participants need to come out winning. Relationships should be mutually beneficial for them to be sustained. You must be ready to give and receive value from a relationship. This implies all participants must add value to each other by leveraging their wealth of experience and acting as a support system in different areas of life—finance, career, wealth, and family. You cannot be in a relationship that is one-sided and expect it to be sustained because as you progress in the relationship, the other party will start feeling the strain of it being one-sided.

Ifeoma and Shade were friends in the university. After graduation, Ifeoma worked for an organization with global presence across multiple countries, where she grew through the ranks to become a senior manager while Shade became a lecturer. Twenty years later, Shade is a lecturer, consulting for multiple organizations and structuring a new business in data science, focused on using data and analytics to generate actionable insights for businesses. Because of her experience in the global organization, Ifeoma is able to offer support to Shade. Meanwhile, Shade provides Ifeoma with technical know-how in data science, an area where she is currently a consultant. If their relationship was one-sided, it would have been short-lived.

The only way a relationship can last is to make sure you give and not only focus on taking. To nurture relationships, you need to be sure you are giving value.

Be Accountable: Accountability is key for nurturing healthy relationships. Everyone plays different roles in relationships and your performance today determines the outcome of future engagements. If you deliver a task today, it will be easy to recommend you when opportunities come up in future. A colleague who was a development engineer showed exceptional qualities, delivered well in his job duties and was always ready to go the extra mile. 7 years down the line, he got an opportunity to offer his services to a bigger conglomerate. This opportunity was based on referral from his former colleagues who had visibility into his previous performance. If he had not exhibited great qualities, he would not have been considered for the available position. Be ready to hold yourself accountable.

iv. There is Value to be Gained

Benefits or value accrue to you if you connect with people through communication and empathy. These benefits come in different forms and can take the form of immediate or long-term returns. Defining your goal for connecting with others will help shape your expectations.

Recommendation: Value provided will lead to recommendations. How are your services recommended to prospective clients? What is spoken about your personality, attitude, and work ethic? Based on your performance, past work experiences, or interactions, referrals are made. Requests for a recommendation can bring both positive and negative feedback. Sometime ago, I called someone who was listed as a reference by a new recruit. To my surprise, the feedback I received was that the candidate did not display accountability at his previous job, rather he took pleasure in bossing people without following through to ensure the task was completed. When required, he was not ready to get his hands dirty. This kind of feedback can be a setback in the recruitment process. A friend was appointed to resume at a multinational telecommunications organization and before resumption, people within the new organization had sourced for information across the industry checking on character, work ethics and so many other attitudes that we do not consider important. The use of standard solutions across the industry requires the need to know the vendors, solution providers and members of various organizations within the industry. This informal reference check was done across the players within the industry. They were eagerly waiting for the new boss based on the recommendations from all the previous engagement, the individual had left an indelible mark in people's lives.

Relationships are crucial and can evolve from mere acquaintances to one that adds great value. You therefore need to choose how you want a relationship to evolve and deliberately work towards that goal.

Support System: Building a support system is critical as you progress in your career. A support system consists of a group of people you can always rely on. They can act as a soundboard and assist you in handling some responsibilities when you need additional support or when you need to focus on a particular area. They are people in your corner who watch out for your best interest, listen to you, and provide honest feedback. Some of the benefits you derive from a great support system include, improved well-being, greater opportunity to de-stress, better ability to focus on goals and achieve results, better coping skills, a well-balanced life, and a shorter journey to accomplishing your goals by leveraging their wealth of experience.

You need to determine what you need from a support system. Are you looking for a friend that you can confide in and who can help you unwind, do you need family to help with some parental responsibilities while you focus on your career, do you need someone to assist with household chores so you can channel your energy to other priorities or do you want to upgrade your professional career? Whatever your needs, it is important to build a support system with a broad base, covering different areas, depending on your goals. At different times, I have leveraged on family members and childcare institutions as support system for childcare, either when I need to work late or attend to duties outside the home. Outsourcing some responsibilities is another way to balance us and leverage support. The need to be creative is important. Your support system can consist of family, friends, and people from your professional network and faith-based communities, and so on. It is also good to start with people you know, especially family and friends. Be willing to ask for help. Your support system are the people who will pull you up when times get tough. Invest in them by strengthening existing relationships and be strategic and deliberate in nurturing them.

Mentors and Sponsors: You can connect with mentors and sponsors. A mentor will guide you on a career path based on your career goals. A mentor is more experienced than you are and might or might not be working in your organization. On the other hand, a sponsor can be a senior colleague within your organization, who can speak for you behind closed doors. A sponsor will champion your cause to ensure you are visible. As a professional, it is important to decide if you require either one of the two. However, having both mentors and sponsors has merits for shaping your professional and life journey. Mentors can help you develop your career path. Sponsors can make you visible, introducing you to their circle of influence, whom you might otherwise not have access to. Mentors and sponsors are advantageous for growth.

Mentors and sponsors can seek to connect with you based on performance and interactions. If you are a top performer, don't be surprised when senior colleagues become mentors or sponsors without you soliciting their involvement in your career. There are also instances where you need to seek out this set of people as you progress on your journey. At different times in my career, I have been fortunate to have both mentors and sponsors, most of whom I did not deliberately go looking for. They sought me out based on my work performance and people skills. If a relationship with a senior employee is mutually beneficial it can culminate in mentorship or sponsorship.

v. Key Reflections

Be prepared to build and leverage relationships, all of which requires trust as well as these key considerations

- Willingness to connect with people through empathy, developing genuine interest in people and showing appreciation
- Influence through associations and interactions that align with your goals.
- Treasure and nurture these relationships and settle differences using crucial conversations approach as you navigate your way
- Adopt a win-win model for mutual benefits, these relationships cannot be one sided

CHAPTER 9
REFLECT AND DOCUMENT BY JOURNALING

It is good to journal your thoughts, feelings, and the events of the day because journaling provides an opportunity to reflect on all that is happening around you. By doing this, you will be able to appreciate and evaluate your journey. Journaling provides an avenue to be more grateful, especially because your reflections will help you realize that you are blessed and have had many positive developments occur. It also helps you review and understand where there are gaps for improvements. Journaling can be done in different ways, for example, either on paper or digitally. You can use journals or notepads, or the note app on your phone or digital device if you cannot take your journal along with you all the time. Learning to pause and reflect is a humbling experience. Ten to thirty minutes of reflection can make a huge difference. There is always some progress to recognize daily, even on challenging days.

How often should you do a journal? Your reflection time can be scheduled for the end of each day or spontaneously in the day. If you document spontaneously, you might forget some of the little things that matter. Documenting at the end of the day enables you to reflect on all the happenings of the day, and any feelings or thoughts you had during the day. You can choose to document the five most important things that happened. In the words of Alan Cohen, "There is virtue in work and there is virtue in rest. Use both and overlook neither."

i. Be Appreciative of Your Journey

Through journaling, you become appreciative of your journey, which helps you to avoid regrets and instead see events as lessons or improvement opportunities. When you appreciate your journey, you will validate yourself, let go of bitterness, and build more confidence in your capabilities. When I started documenting the top five things in the categories of family, career, personal, health, and spiritual, that I was grateful for, on a monthly basis, I realized there was a lot to be grateful for. By not reflecting, I was not able to fully quantify how much value has been added, to myself and family, and could not fully recognize the many blessings I had benefited from. By doing this exercise, I became more informed about the areas that I needed to focus on, and I was able to celebrate my wins. I had never even assigned value to most of my wins because I had not taken time to reflect on them. Documenting my journey enabled me to better enjoy myself and rid myself of complaints as I realized that there were many things to appreciate in life.

Plan Better and Achieve Results: You can plan better. Reflecting on your journey gives you room to stay focused and avoid distractions. By documenting your journey, you can see what you have achieved and what is yet to be achieved. When you start connecting the dots, you are better able to set a vision for the future. Envisioning the future is a key step to succeeding in life. Once you can envision your future, commit to its execution. Tracking your execution plan is important. Reflecting and documenting are the best ways to track your progress.

This can be applied to any area of life. You can decide to document your fitness journey for a healthy lifestyle. Documenting your food intake daily for one month helps you evaluate your eating habits to determine if there are specific measures that you need to imbibe to improve health and wellness. Studies show that people, who documented their daily food intake for a week, ended up losing twice more calories than those who did not. Documenting your daily actions helps you identify what takes up much of your time. If you document all your activities on a daily or weekly basis, you will have enough data to understand your daily life patterns. A review of these activities may highlight that you spend 80% of your time on specific activities that are work-related or fun. It is your responsibility to evaluate your findings and determine if they align with your goals. If they do not, you can develop a plan of action to change this. This habit can guide your focus and achievements in any area of life.

Celebrate Wins: Most times, we do not celebrate our wins because we are waiting for the really big wins before we celebrate. Unfortunately, we can wait endlessly if nothing we do seems like a big win. You can have small wins, which you can categorize as a set of steps required to achieve a goal that is a big win. An example of this is writing a book, which is a big win. Writing a book requires steps such as committing time to write and writing the chapters. You can celebrate these small wins. Another example is completing an industry certification course. Planning and starting the preparation process are wins. Reading course materials and taking various assessment tests before the actual certification are small wins that aid the overall goal of attaining a favorable score for the certification. This can also be likened to buying a house, where putting aside monthly savings geared towards achieving this goal are part of small wins that can be celebrated.

Reflecting gives you an avenue to acknowledge and celebrate your wins, no matter how small. Celebration does not have to be done in grand style. A pat on the back, time out with family or alone, or a visit to the spa or movies, is enough to celebrate. With the recent trend of building an online presence, you could consider a post on any of your platforms to celebrate with your connections. Tracking and acknowledging small and incremental wins will create bigger wins. These actions create a boost in motivation and self-confidence.

Humbling Experience: Learning to pause and reflect is a humbling experience. I have a 'goals workbook' where I document my goals for the year. Reflecting on the goals in this workbook allows me to track my progress, acknowledge my achievements, and determine the goals to focus on.

Some people paste pictures of their goals and plans on vision boards, to guide their daily thoughts and actions. Recall my example of leading the delivery of a vision board for a department within an organization. This was extensively discussed in Chapter 1. The vision board was designed to show the state of technology transformation in the next 5 years and it was delivered in print and video. Placing this in a strategic location for everyone to see daily provided the insight and motivation to ensure the set ambitions are achieved. Vision boards aid visualization of your goals and vision, which is a key part of reflecting and documenting. While reflecting, signals are sent to the brain that what is being reflected on is important, and the brain therefore drives focus for execution.

How to Journal: There is no particular way to reflect. Each individual has a unique style that can evolve over time. The first step is to start writing, no matter how little and gradually improve with time. Your process has to come naturally too; there is no point copying what other people are doing. Identify your unique process and stick with it.

ii. Journaling Helps You Live a Better Life

Keeping a journal is a way to document and record ideas or concepts visualized. Idea generation is unique for each individual and can occur in different ways. For some people, observing a quiet time births idea while for others, ideas can spring up at any time of the day. Whichever way ideas are generated, it is important to document them to avoid forgetting them. Reflecting on these ideas will set you on course to start building a plan to execute and ensure they become reality.

It Reduces Stress: Reflecting on your thoughts, feelings, and actions reduces stress. A study shows that journaling for fifteen to twenty minutes a day, over a period of four months, can lower blood pressure and improve liver functionality. Can you imagine the health benefits that accrue from reflecting? The study is insightful and further stresses the importance of reflecting and documenting. Reflecting can also boost your mood. A review of a great day can boost your mood, inspiring you to achieve more. Reflecting through journaling will boost your comprehension and memory capacity. Your memory is also kept fresh as you have many things at the forefront of your mind. Reflecting gives you fresh perspectives as you review your journey so that you are better able to make sense of your thoughts and experiences. Reflecting helps you become organized in meaningful ways and helps you manage stressful experiences in a healthy way.

Living a better life through journaling allows you to record your ideas and concepts for easy reference and use. These ideas can end up becoming the next big thing.

iii. Myths and Misconceptions of Documenting

Reflecting and documenting offer many benefits. However, there are myths and misconceptions associated with documenting your thoughts, feelings, actions, and plans. Some of these myths and misconceptions, although real, can be negated by having proper plans in place and by considering the immense benefits of reflecting and documenting your journey.

Privacy Concerns: A foremost concern revolves around privacy and the fear of malicious access to what has been documented. This is a valid concern and as a responsible individual, you need to put a plan in place to avoid this. Your reflections can be documented in paper form, using journals or notepads, or it can be done digitally or online, using a writing, note-taking, or journaling app on your mobile phone. It is important to secure access to the documentation; whatever format is used. Security features such as two-factor authentication can be used for digital documentation or on your phone.

Not Having Enough Time: If it is important to you, you will create time for it, and no amount of time is small. Schedule time consistently, either daily, weekly, or monthly, to reflect and document. The power of consistency is a key contributing factor because it helps you improve and plan your time better creating time to journal. Five minutes a day is good enough as a start. I used to complain that I did not have time for reflection and journaling. However, recent experiences of journaling have enabled me to identify its value and I now create time for it.

There have been occasions when I was at an event and some thoughts ran through my mind. I immediately picked up my phone and started the journaling process.

Fear of Reliving Memories: Reliving memories can be both good and bad. People shy away from recalling ugly memories for fear of arousing uncleared hurt. Sometimes, reflecting on and journaling ugly experiences can stir emotions. Being deliberate in recalling these memories will allow you to let go of the situation and learn your lessons. It offers you an opportunity to objectively determine what went well in that experience and what requires improvement. If relieving memories gives you a traumatic experience, it is important to seek professional support from qualified medical personnel.

iv. Key Reflections

Journaling is good, it enables you to reflect, gives you fresh views, and appreciate your journey. You can journal thoughts, ideas, feelings and events.

- Define what, when and how you want to journal
- See it as a gratifying process
- Create and schedule time to journal
- Understand the myths and misconceptions of journaling
- Live a better life well equipped with ideas

CHAPTER 10
NO EXPERIENCE IS WASTED

The experiences we have in life are events and connections that leave an impression on us. This includes our day-to-day interactions with different people as we journey in life. These experiences occur within family circles, the workplace, faith-based organizations, community, and all walks of life. They could leave a sweet or sour taste when we reflect on them, depending on our impressions from such experiences. Experiences define life in its totality, and we must learn to embrace each day and the experiences that come with it.

i. Each Experience Has a Learning Point

Do you know that no experience is wasted? Every experience counts and is a part of your journey. All our experiences contain lessons. Each experience will either grow or shape you. Experience in all areas of life can be viewed from different perspectives. It can be seen as a training ground to prepare you for greater and higher levels of responsibilities; especially if it gives you room to stretch. Reflecting recently on my undergraduate experience showed me that I was being prepared to be solution minded. As physics undergraduates, almost everyone in my department wanted to change their course of study from physics to a seemingly more lucrative course such as computer science. We believed that physics graduates ended up as teachers. Unknown to us, we were being prepared. Most of us could not change our course of study, and we ended up graduating as physicists. Some of my classmates now practice computer science as a profession while others have gone on to various roles and industries. During our undergraduate years, I was part of the committee that delivered our final-year newsletter. Fourteen years later, I was championing a newsletter within an organization as publisher and lead editor – dealing with production and circulation. My experience of working on a newsletter at university, served me well. Combining that with today's technology, my team and I delivered a first-of-its-kind newsletter to the organization.

We often do not acknowledge and embrace all our experiences. It is good to be appreciative of your journey irrespective of the complexities surrounding each phase. Note that tough times don't last, only tough people do. Our experiences are training grounds to challenge and motivate us to aspire and become better versions of ourselves.

A Launch Pad to Support Others: Experience can also be a launch pad to support others. Share your experiences to help others overcome the kind of issues you have encountered. You can make the journey shorter for others. Some of the experiences can include, dealing with a difficult boss and colleagues, and combining work and family while ensuring there is room for personal care, which is work-life balance or work-life integration. They could also be around commute time and the fact that you spend too much time commuting to work due to various reasons. These are common challenges that we all have to deal with at different phases of life. Dealing with these challenging situations and working through them puts you in a position to share your experiences and support others on their growth journey. There are people who tried to study for a master's degree program while working full time, and they had to drop off along the way. If you have weathered and pulled through this stage successfully, achieving additional qualifications or a master's while working, sharing your journey with others will guide and help them work through the challenges. They will realize that they are not the first and they will not be the last to combine working with studying. Equipping others with this knowledge will help prospective protégés to deal with the issues and proactively put in measures to avoid them. These experiences, shared as stories, serve as learning opportunities through which mentoring and coaching support are offered to others. The value in this can best be appreciated by people who have benefited from such experiences.

Your Reaction Matters: Your reactions to experiences determine the outcome you see. If a positive outcome is desired, adopt a positive reaction even when the experience is not as expected. Imagine that you are someone who always exceeds expectations and gives your best to deliver tasks assigned to you. What if your efforts are neither visible nor appreciated by your immediate boss, will you then stop giving your best? No, doing this will affect your performance and brand. The best approach is to find out why your work is not appreciated and develop key steps to improve your work and create visibility for the right audience. Choose your reactions, reflect, and be deliberate about how you respond. This will shape the experiences you encounter.

ii. Define Your Journey

Our journey in life is unique and shaped by experiences, values, actions, thoughts, and our purpose. In charting a path for the future, it is crucial that you define your journey.

Discover Your Why: Why are you on this journey? Discover your why. Find consistent themes on your journey and let your values be seen throughout the journey. Understand that your journey is distinct, so you cannot compare yourself with others. In my undergraduate class at university, we were fifty, and it's obvious as I reflect on where we are today, twenty years after we left school, that our journeys are not the same. We have taken different career paths in various industries. This also applies to my classmates from secondary school. In life we will all evolve. There is no need to allow envy set in.

Sometime ago, a former colleague was promoted to vice president, Africa for a prestigious multinational firm. I was tempted to begin comparing because we started our career journey as engineers within the same organization. However, as I reflect on that period, I am convinced that everyone has a different path in life, and we are not all moving at the same pace. Your evolution will differ depending on experiences on your journey. Our journeys are unique, and we need to learn to embrace each phase.

iii. Embrace Each Phase to Grow and Shape You

Embrace each phase of your journey. Your experiences will either grow you or shape you. Growing through a phase requires an open mind, knowing that all your experiences will be useful as you progress in life. Over the course of my career, I have had to go through diverse experiences, some of which were painful and challenging at the time.

Remember my experience that I described in chapter 4, where I had to prepare without warning to make a presentation on new technologies and the corresponding culture shift. Going through the painful process of having to stay up late to prepare for the session and receiving positive feedback after the presentation, helped me to value the importance of determination in achieving goals. The knowledge acceleration sessions I led for various organizations and my career experiences, both in my early years and as I rose up the career ladder, were springboards to whom I have become today. The projects I have handled over the years and the support provided to me were instrumental to the growth I experienced. Most of these experiences are now being used in different contexts.

Our experiences shape who we become. How do you pass through life? Looking back now, I see that the tough times I faced were preparing me for the future. Most of my painful experiences have shaped me. Being on a lower cadre(level?) today is not the end of the world, rather it is a phase to enjoy, embrace, and maximize. Embrace each phase irrespective of your experiences, either positive or negative, as it serves as the bedrock to greater achievements in life.

iv. Your Experiences can Serve as a Mark of Credibility

Your experiences can serve as a mark of credibility if you have been successful in achieving visible results as you progress in your life and career. Have you interacted with different individuals from all walks of life? How have those experiences ended? Were they value-adding or did they end in bitterness? Irrespective of how these experiences unfolded, adding value to people will attract the attention of others because most people will see your success without knowing the great and painful experiences you went through. Therefore, you can showcase your brand through your experiences. In defining your journey, you will discover your why and this discovery will assist in shaping your brand, which if followed through, will build credibility. Credibility requires you to be trusted and believed. This credibility is earned through engagement with other people. Having credibility makes you attractive to sponsors and mentors; either solicited or unsolicited, through the value you create because everyone wants to associate with success.

v. Key Reflections

Your experiences are not wasted, they grow or shape you on your journey. There is a need to view all experiences with different perspectives. It can be seen as a training ground if it stretches you. Challenging experiences are learning opportunities. They have learnings to grow you to become better prepared for new opportunities and from these experiences you can coach or support others. Learn to embrace and treasure each phase in life. Key considerations

- Each experience has a learning point
- Define your journey and understand your why. Your journey is unique to you
- Embrace each phase and make the best of it. It will grow and shape you
- Your experiences can serve as a mark of credibility and attract mentors and sponsors

CHAPTER 11
LEAD FROM THE HEART
ANYWHERE YOU ARE

We all have so much greatness in us and do not realize this. We are often limited by our beliefs, some of which have been ingrained in us with or without our knowledge. By becoming more self-aware and conscious of things that are normally in your subconscious, you can ignite the leader within you. Wake up to this reality and stir up the leader within you. You can lead from the heart, anywhere you are, in the corporate world, on an entrepreneurial journey, or life in general.

Leading is influence. It is the ability to influence an individual's behavior, thoughts, and actions. Your ability to influence your environment is a key part of leadership. Most times, we influence the behavior of others around us without realizing it. Our actions, whether positive or negative, influence others and a deliberate focus is required to ensure that we portray leadership qualities as we go about our daily journey in life. Leading is not about your position. Not being the boss does not mean you are not a leader. As long as you are able to motivate others to achieve a goal or make a change, you are leading. This applies to our homes, offices, churches, and any other setting, if the definition fits. You can lead from any part of the organization.

There are key shifts that need to happen to an individual as he or she embraces this process. Most of these are daily actions that we do not take cognizance of. The mindset shift that we discussed earlier plays a huge role here. In chapter one, we discussed shifting perspectives and shaping your mind, which are critical to progress in life. These attitudes are a deviation from being cautious, and they embrace learning to take some risks. Through this process, you learn to become a better person each day. These shifts can be intentionally planned and introduced into every aspect of life.

i. It Starts With a Step

It starts with a step. Determine that you want to lead and start by taking a step forward.

Do Not Overthink and Complicate Things: Overthinking complicates things. Once you have an idea or thought, you need to take a step to implement it, this will be a trigger for execution. Assuming that you can think through every plan in detail is unrealistic and the longer you delay actualizing your plan, the greater the probability that you will never fulfil it. Recall my story about setting up a WhatsApp group for my secondary school and university alumni. I was not in touch with most of my former classmates and this could have hindered me from taking action. Instead, I created the group with only four people and asked them to add other classmates that they were in contact with. Within a short while, we had about 200 former classmates in the group, some of whom had not been in contact with others for twenty years, and they were spread across the world. This was a fulfilling experience. Start with a step and work it out along the way.

My moving to Liberia was another journey of not overcomplicating things. With an opportunity to move to a new country and stretch beyond my comfort zone, some concerned friends expressed their fears. There were questions as to if I was sure I should be taking up this new opportunity, how will I navigate the journey balancing family life and work. While I had my fears, I did not let these comments deter me. I had a high-level plan of how to balance family life and work, however this was not fully developed. As you know, you cannot think through all the various situations that can play out. I equally had a plan of creating time for other value adding initiatives depending on how things progress. There were a lot of ideas on my mind. Reflecting on this journey less than 2 years after, it has been an incredible journey, full of self-discovery and evolution. I have been transformed through the journey and become more aware of my capabilities. The initial plan I had, is also evolving on the journey, there has been work life integration with visible patterns and results of my capabilities. My initial capabilities after careful consideration prepared me to take a decision to progress on this journey which has now advanced beyond the original plan. Being on the journey gives opportunity to practice to become better.

Practice to Become Better: Experiences are had by doing. It is only when you do something that you can confirm that you have experience in that area. Even if your goal was not achieved, passing through the journey is an experience. It is therefore important to be more interested in acquiring practice through the journey of executing an idea than to complicate it with overthinking. This does not mean planning should be discarded. You need to plan, but do not complicate the plan. Also, make room for contingencies. You cannot think through everything.

Measure Progress: As you take the step, you need to monitor your progress. Progress refers to some advancement towards your goal. It therefore means you need to define a goal, which you can measure your progress against. Your progress needs to be monitored and evaluated, and this can start with documenting it. When you reflect, you generate fresh insights that would have gone unnoticed due to much busyness. By doing this, you are able to gather new insights to assess how far you have moved and your successes so far and reconsider your existing plans for improvement. Measuring progress serves as a motivation to continue towards your goal, especially when you realize that you have made achievements, no matter how small. These achievements might have otherwise gone unnoticed if progress was not evaluated.

Celebrate Little Achievements: It is important to celebrate the milestone achievements and the little achievements. By celebrating achievements, no matter how small, you gain confidence to move forward and achieve more. Celebrating makes you proud and inspires you to do more. Your celebration does not have to be grand. It can be as simple as taking a short break, writing yourself a gratitude note, or having a shout out on social media. Sometimes you could post a nice picture on social media celebrating your achievement, and just enjoy the comments and banter that might follow. Some others might go to a faith-filled environment to offer thanksgiving to God. You can decide to celebrate in your own way as there is no one-size-fits-all method. It is dependent on your taste and preferences.

If you are on a journey to becoming a top-notch professional in your field, a first step to increasing your experience and exposure could be making a presentation to the executive committee of your organization or the board of directors. If you are on a journey to complete a master's degree program, your first step is registering for the course before you gradually navigate your way to completion, not forgetting to celebrate on the way. Starting with one step is how to execute your ideas. As you progress on the journey, you learn at each phase, become better than you were at the beginning, and generate many more ideas that will culminate into growing your leadership.

ii. Do it Afraid

In planning and executing your ideas, you will have fears, especially when you are transiting into the unknown or making bold decisions like, moving to a new industry or organization, and taking up a new role. You will have doubts. Deal with doubts by facing your fears, you do not need to act on the fear. You need courage to achieve your dreams. Courage is the ability to do something that frightens you. This courage will be required continually. Do not be afraid to be a beginner. We are all learning and growing each day.

Face Your Fears: Facing your fears grows and shapes you for new challenges. These challenges will birth new experiences, which shapes your journey. Sometime ago, an organization structural change moved me across departments. There were fears of how the new structure will be shaped as it was anticipated this will be a disadvantage for me and my team. Despite the fears, the change progressed, and I had to develop courage to face the challenges most of which was inevitable. We were new within the environment and the other department already had a way of working and structure. There were some processes that were not a focus area for my team which we needed to adjust to. Some of these changes seemed insurmountable. Over time, we adjusted to the environment, started learning new ways of work with need for extensive documentation and processes. We came out better for it, as the final structure was much better than expected.

Another case was my move to Liberia as described above was stated as a bold move by one of my colleagues. It was a new environment, I knew no one there and my portfolio was expanded in terms of scope of work. I was going to be away from family for a while. There were so many fears however I continued with courage. It was tough with need to fully understand the environment, transform the team and ensure we deliver great success. A transformation plan was developed, and implementation commenced to achieve the goal. There was a need to be adaptable as execution progressed to address disruptions on the way. I made sure the team was actively engaged and aligned with the plan through constant communication and engagement. I reflect now and am quite happy that I took that step as my life has fully transformed.

Some key steps to addressing fears are to identify the fear, own the fear, visualize past achievements, and chart a way forward. Move with courage to achieve your goals.

iii. Lead Yourself

To be able to influence others, you need to lead yourself. Everything we do in life involves others. Our ability to influence others and ourselves is the differentiating factor. To lead yourself, you must be self-motivated and have self-direction. You need to hold yourself accountable to a set of personal values, beliefs, and goals. Act with integrity even when no one is looking.

Self-Motivation is Important: You must be internally motivated, not waiting for people to push you to achieve more. To be self-motivated means that you continue to push yourself to make progress even with challenges. Although any number of excuses may come up on the way, you need to be determined.

Prioritize Personal Growth Over Everything: You constantly have to seek knowledge to develop yourself. Distractions may come in the form of people; however, once you prioritize your personal growth, no matter what is happening, you will stay focused. Personal growth requires continuous development to reach your full potential. You need to be hungry to grow yourself because life is all about living, learning, and growing. To experience growth, you need to make it a priority, not giving room for excuses.

I recall a time when a senior colleague told me, during a meeting, that we needed to create time for personal development. I responded that work was demanding, therefore I could not create the time. His response shocked me. He informed me that I should be passionate about my development as much as my work, and I should make sure I created time for it. Looking back over the years, I really appreciate that moment of truth because it helped shape my thirst for personal development.

Live Your Values: Living your values is equally important. It is important to define your values because defining your values serve as the foundation for living them out. Defining your values will shape what is important to you. Knowing your values requires reflecting on your past and your responses to situations. What values have you felt good about exhibiting?

These then become the crucial values that you can intentionally plan to continue living out. As a leader, your values form your core and guide all actions you take. When everything around you fails or when challenges occur, you tend to withdraw, and your values are the foundation that then shapes your actions.

Learn to Dream Big: A leader needs to be able to dream and dream big. Your ability to dream and pursue your dreams is central to leading yourself. Everyone can have dreams and aspirations, however your execution and success in achieving them differentiates you from others. Do not be afraid to dream big and execute well.

One of my leaders had very big audacious dreams and did not hesitate to share this at every opportunity. As the world was transforming, he predicted the need to get ready to advance and transform key functions to become a gateway to the world and not just continue to operate locally within a market. He gave no room for doubts to suppress these thoughts and by sharing with others, he was gradually building them as accountability partners. All his connections who hear his dreams will want to watch out to see it materialize and since he has publicly announced this, he was equally committed to follow through. With his team, work began, there were many stops on the way due to conflicting priorities and the need to continue running as usual versus getting ready for the future. He stayed committed because he believed in his vision. Fast forward 6 years now, we see the vision materialize and can all see the results of what was stated as dreams. The organization is ready to adopt new technologies due to the level of preparedness that had happened. The actualization also projects him as a thoughtful and visionary leader. As at the time he commenced, the final output did not look real. The deliverables which seemed unachievable and audacious some years ago is very much aligned with recent global trends and addresses market needs.

Become Self-directed: Self-direction is the ability to make your own decisions and organize your work rather than someone directing you regarding what to do. As a self-motivator, you need to direct yourself. You need to set goals, take initiative when required, not waiting to be told to take an action, prioritize great work, and be a solution provider. These qualities will ensure you are directing yourself. If you do not set goals, you will end up wandering through the year, dealing with irrelevant things without achieving anything. Setting goals helps shape your mind, thoughts, and actions. Taking the initiative and prioritizing great work are key traits of a leader. Exceeding expectations is how you prioritize great work. When something is wrong, take the initiative and chart a way forward.

Become a Solution Provider: Be a solution provider, someone who is ready to always find answers and fix problems. Being solution-oriented requires an optimistic approach that is constantly looking for ways to solve problems even when everyone else is focused on the challenges. Looking for better ways of doing things and interrupting unhelpful thinking are some of the qualities that differentiate leaders. While others are lamenting about problems, you should step up and proffer solutions.

iv. Adapt and Lead Change

You must be ready to adapt and to lead change. In life, there will be detours, challenges and opportunities, unchartered territories, disruptions, and so on. Our approach to adaptation and to change is critical. To lead change, you need to be adaptable and resilient.

Be Adaptable: Being adaptable is defined by how easy it is to adjust to new and uncertain conditions. Unfavorable conditions are not desired; however, they will occur at different times. At the beginning of 2020, people had their goals mapped out until the Coronavirus (COVID-19) pandemic happened. The entire world was at a standstill, airports, businesses, and the economy shut down in view of the infectious disease. Most people's plans were immediately impacted, and losses were recorded across various industries. Plans that had been set as goals for execution were immediately affected. There is a need for a balance between built-to-last and built-to-adapt. Therefore, people had to adjust their plan to the current realities.

I was scheduled to attend John Maxwell International Maxwell Certification but due to the pandemic, it was initially postponed indefinitely. When the organizers realized that the pandemic was not going to end soon, the summit was converted to a virtual event, and guess what, it became the virtual event of the year. Many individuals benefited from the summit, including those that had wanted to attend the physical session over the years, but had not been able to. The virtual version presented an opportunity for the summit organizers to have a wider audience.

How adaptable are you? Are you built to last or built to adapt? When uncertainties and disruptions occur, do you just fold your arms, believing nothing can be done? A leader must be willing to adapt his plans as the tide changes. We live in a complex environment that can be uncertain, unpredictable, and vague. I joined an organization expecting to spend two years, but I ended up spending over fourteen years. I could have mourned the fact that I had spent longer than I planned and not bothered to give my best. However, I continued to give my best and offer value, and my progress has been transforming. The transformation might not have occurred as I planned, but the need to remain adaptable far overshadowed my initial goal. This is how to remain adaptable and keep moving forward despite uncertainties. As a leader, you need to be ready for uncertain times because they will come. Your core values matter, and you need to remain adaptable.

Be Resilient: The previous discussion on being adaptable brings us to resilience. How resilient are you? How quickly can you recover from challenges or difficulties? That is what defines your resilience. Do you buckle when challenges occur? There is no need to do that. As we make progress, unexpected turns or challenges will occur, and we must be ready to embrace them and push forward. A resilient leader will keep forging ahead despite obstacles, and this is what differentiates and sets you apart.

Following the organization-wide restructure that was mentioned in chapter ten, there were two concerns. One, was the change that was initially anticipated to turn bad which ended up turning positively in our favor, the other bit is the volume of work required to be fulfilled immediately the restructure was completed. Due to the need to align to new ways of working, the three-man team set to work, to begin settling in to the new department. A few months into this, one of the team members resigned for greener pastures. We were the only two people remaining to deliver the huge volume of work pending his replacement. It was a transition state, and the new structure was still being finalized in the new environment. There was fear of team collapse and now we had to deal with being overworked. This was overwhelming; however, we did not suck up complaining, rather we went to work taking the delivery in bits. Brainstormed on ideas and sought opportunities to get someone from another department to support which was successful. Gradually we began achieving results, although this was not at the optimal level until the final structure was concluded.

This phase taught us resilience. As we reflect now, we realize that we were learning about resilience and adaptability in that season. Resilient leaders can stand the test of time and will not buckle under pressure. While we do not want to constantly work under pressure, there will be instances where we have to stretch, and we need to be prepared.

Becoming the best version of yourself requires that you ignite the leader within you, and then everyone will know you for delivering great value, which will differentiate you from others. Success is achievable, but it requires hard work and intentional living.

You need to own your stuff, own your space, own your success, and your worth. Believe in yourself, uncover your true potential, celebrate yourself, know your name, and name your price. Being resilient gives you an opportunity to reinvent yourself and give yourself the opportunity to shine. There is nothing limiting you. You are filled with greatness and are unstoppable. It is through learning and practical experiences that leaders are made.

v. Key Reflections

You can lead from the heart, anywhere you are, as a career person, an entrepreneur and irrespective of your profession. This extends to life in general. Influencing your environment, people's behaviors, thoughts and actions are all part of leadership. An intentional effort is required to exhibit leadership qualities in your daily interactions. Key considerations instrumental to succeeding have been discussed extensively. They are.

- Decide you want to lead, start with a step, don't over think it and practice to become better
- Do it afraid, identify the fear, learn to face your fears, visualize your past achievements and develop courage
- Lead yourself through personal development, dream big, be a solution provider
- Be ready to adapt and lead change. This requires you to be resilient and adaptable

REFERENCES:

https://restless.co.uk/health/healthy-mind/the-power-of-journaling-as-a-life-habit/

(Chapter 9, How to Reduce Stress)